# Hot Springs

# of

# Northern California

*by*

George Williams III

**TBR Trust**
P.O. Box 191
Genoa, Nevada 89411
1 (775) 887-1394 or 1(775)750-8646
To order books visit: **www.hotspringguides.com**

Hot Springs of Northern California
2nd Revised Edition
By George Williams III

Published by:
**TBR Trust**
P.O. Box 191
Genoa, Nevada 89411
To order books  call 1-775-887-1394 or go to **www.hotspringguides.com**

Cover photo of one of  the deeps pools at Keough's Hot Spring Ditch, Bishop, California. The author gives praise to He who created the geothermal waters.

*"...whoever drinks the water I give him will never thirst. Indeed, the water I give him will become in him a spring of water welling up to eternal life."* John 4:14

Other non-fiction books by George Williams III:
**Hot Springs of Nevada (1996)**
**Hot Springs of the Eastern Sierra (4th revised ed. 2000 )**
**In the Last of the Wild West (1992  revised 1999)**
**The Guide To Bodie and Eastern Sierra Historic Sites (1981)**
**Rosa May: The Search For A Mining Camp Legend (1979)**
**The Redlight Ladies Of Virginia City, Nevada (1984)**
**The Murders At Convict Lake (1984)**
**On the Road with Mark Twain in  California and Nevada (1994)**
**Mark Twain: His Adventures At Aurora and Mono Lake (1987)**
**Mark Twain:  His Life In Virginia City, Nevada (1986)**
**Mark Twain and The Jumping Frog of Calaveras County (1989)**
**The Songwriter's Demo Manual  and Success Guide (1984 revised 2000))**
**Repair Your Credit (2001)**

# Table of Contents

Author's Introduction                          6
Locating Hot Springs                           8
Hot Spring Etiquette                           8
Camping at Hot Springs                         9
Equipment Needed                               9
When Can Hot Springs Be Reached               10
Caution: Be Careful                           10


1. Surprise Valley Hot Springs, Cedarville    11
2. Leonard Hot Spring, Cedarville             14
3. Glen Hot Spring, Cedarville                15
4. Eagleville Hot Spring, Eagleville          16
5. Wild Mint Hot Spring, Eagleville           18
6. Big Bend Hot Springs, Big Bend             19
7. Woody's Feather River Hot Spring, Quincy   21
8. Sierra Hot Springs, Sierraville            22
9. Wilbur Hot Springs, Williams               23
10. Vichy Hot Springs Resort and Inn, Ukiah   25
11. Orr Hot Springs, Ukiah                    29
12. Harbin Hot Springs, Middletown            31

Calistoga Hot Spring Resorts                  33
13. Golden Haven Hot Springs                  33
14. Calistoga Village Inn and Spa             34
15. Indian Springs                            35
16. Dr. Wilkinson's Hots Springs Resort       38
17. Roman Spa Hot Springs Resort              38
18. Eurospa and Inn                           39
19. Calistoga Spa Hot Springs                 40
20. Nances Hot Springs                        41
21. Sonoma Mission Inn and Spa, Sonoma        42
22. White Sulphur Springs, St. Helena         42
23. Grover Hot Springs, Markleeville          44
24. East Carson Hot Springs#1                 45
25. East Carson Hot Springs #2                49

Bridgeport Hot Springs                        50
26. Fales Hot Spring Ditch                    50
27. Big Hot                                   51
28. Travertine Hot Spring                     52

29. Buckeye Hot Spring                        55

**Mono Lake Hot  Springs**                    57
30. Dechambeau Ranch Hot Spring               57
31. Navy Beach Hot Spring                     58
32. Paoha Island Hot Spring                   61

**Mammoth Lakes Hot Springs**                 61
33. Red's Meadow Hot Spring                   61
34. Fish Creek Hot Spring                      63

**Long Valley Hot Springs
(near Mammoth Lakes)**
35. Whitmore Hot Spring                        63
36. Hot Creek                                  65
37. Little Hot Creek                           68
38. Wild Willy's Hot  Spring                   69
39. Hilltop Hot Spring                         71
40. The Tub Hot Spring                         72
41. Shepherd's Hot  Spring                     73
42. Shepherd's #2 Hot Spring                   75
43. The Crab Cooker (Ken's tub)               76
44. The Bath Tub                               77
45. The Pond Hot Spring                        78

46. Old House Benton Hot Springs, Benton      78
47. Keough's Hot Springs, Bishop              80
48. Keough's Hot Spring Ditch, Bishop         82

**Maps**
Hot Springs of Northern California             5
Bridgeport Hot Springs                        54
Long Valley Hot  Springs                       66

**Books by George Williams III**              84
**Autographed Book Order form**               87

## Warning: Disclaimer:

The author here acknowledges and warns readers that hot springs can be dangerous and deadly places. The author encourages the readers of this book to take extreme caution before placing any parts of their bodies in hot springs and to carefully manage children near and in hot springs. The author **does not** encourage any person to trespass on private land. Instead, the author encourages all readers to first ask permission before visiting hot springs located on  private lands.

Oregon

N

▲ Glen & Leonard
Hot Springs

▲ Big Bend
Hot Sp.

Cedarville ● ▲

Surprise Valley
Hot Spring

● Redding

▲

▲ Wilbur H.S.

Eagleville &
Wild Mint

▲ Harbin H.S.

▲ Woody's H.S.

● Middletown

▲ Sierraville H.S.

▲ Orr Hot Spring

▲ E. Carson H.S.

● ▲ Vichy Hot Spring

▲ Grover H.S.

Ukiah

▲ Calistoga
Hot Springs

▲ Fales
Hot Spring

▲ White Sulphur

▲ Sonoma
Hot Spring

Bridgeport ●
Hot Springs

● San
Francisco

Mammoth
Lakes
Hot
Speings

Mono
Lake Hot
Springs

▲

▲

Long Valley ▲
Hot Springs

● Bishop

▲

Keough's Hot
Spring & Ditch

▲ Hot
Springs

● Towns/cities

Nevada

# Author's Introduction

Welcome to the 2nd Revised Edition of *Hot Springs of Northern California*. This is the only complete guide to all northern California recreational hot springs. No other book contains this complete information. This is the third in my series of hot spring guides.

This book covers all recreational hot springs from Bishop in the Owens Valley north to the Oregon border.

In *Hot Springs of Northern California* you will discover the locations of secret hot springs previously known only to locals. And you will find hot springs which are well known and used by many in their search for peace and relaxation.

There are plush resorts like Sonoma Mission Hot Springs near Sonoma, Vichy Hot Springs in Ukiah and the Calistoga hot spring resorts, to the far out primitive and wild hot springs of Cedarville near the Nevada border where thousands of gallons of hot water pour out of the foothills into the desert. There are hot springs here where you can soak for free and camp for free; others are resorts which charge reasonable fees. All these hot springs offer you the mysterious and healing mineral waters that gush up from deep inside Earth.

This book will book will save you a lot of trouble. I have searched up and down northern California seeking only those hot springs usable for soaking. Some hot springs are not included because they are unsafe. Others are not included because they are on private property and not open to the public.

In the Eastern Sierra you will find many hot springs that are located on public lands where you can soak and camp for free. West of the Sierra most of the hot springs are on private property and are operated as resorts.

Road directions and a maps are included to help you find each hot spring easily. You won't find road signs to hot springs out in the sticks, so you'll have to trust my directions. You'll have no trouble finding these out of the way hot springs if you follow my directions. I give you a run down on each hot spring—my 2 cents—which will help you get a feel for what you are in for.

If you enjoy this book, you'll want other books in this series, *Hot*

*Springs of the Eastern Sierra* and *Hot Springs of Nevada*. All my books will come autographed and personally inscribed to you, friends, family or business associates. Please keep these books in mind for gifts for birthdays, Christmas and other special occasions.

If you need more information about these books visit **www.hotspringguides.com,** call **1-775-887-1394,** E mail us at **gjw@aol.com,** or check out the list of books in the back of this book.

If you find a hot spring that is not in this book—one that I have somehow missed, I'd like to know about it. Please write or call me and let me know. I'll send you a Free book for your information.

The information in this book is the most up to date at the time of publication. However, as is often the case, information may change after publication. Readers are encouraged to telephone hot spring resorts for current rates before visiting.

Now listen, when I show up at one of these fabulous hot springs and you're there, the least you can do is buy me a drink or give me your car or something. Have a good time and send me some money whenever you can. U.S. currency preferred.

Happy trails until we meet,

George Williams III
P.O. Box 191
Genoa, Nevada 89411.

## Locating Hot Springs

This book lists hot springs from the north to the south. I have attempted to tie together those hot springs that are near one another so you can visit clusters of hot springs on the same trip.

Though the Table of Contents lists forty-eight hot springs, there are actually more than that included in this book. That's because at some locations you will find more than one hot spring. For instance, at Big Hot near Bridgeport, there are actually six separate pools to bathe in.

## Basic Information Included

For each hot spring I provide its location and accurate road directions, how secluded each spot is for those people who are looking for privacy and intimacy, water temperature when last visited, fee, if any, a photograph of the site and the condition, whether or not a concrete or wooden tub is built and if camping is allowed. I give you my personal opinion of each hot spring. If there is no cement or wooden tub, the sight is listed as primitive. Your feet will get a little mucky at places like this so expect it.

## Hot Spring Etiquette

I have found there is a courtesy code amongst "hot springers," people who thrive on visiting hot springs, particularly hot springs in the sticks. For instance, if you reach a hot spring and a couple or a family are bathing, it is polite to wait for them to finish before entering the hot spring pool. You might leave for a while and come back. People appreciate privacy. You will too.

If there are children at a hot spring, most adults will not bathe nude.

There are some hot springs where clothing is required, like Hot Creek near Mammoth Lakes, and many of the resorts west of the Sierra.

Then there are some hot springs where people ordinarily bathe nude. If you feel uncomfortable about bathing nude with strangers, don't feel obliged. Just because others choose to bathe this way, doesn't mean you have to. If it makes you uncomfortable to bathe with a bathing suit on while others are nude, you can always wait until the other bathers are finished.

It should go without saying, hot springs and the area around them should be kept as clean as possible. Don't drop beer tabs into the pools. Pick up your trash when you leave. Do not infect the pool with human waste of any sort. <u>Do not shampoo or use soap in a pool.</u> Instead, bathe outside the pool and rinse off with a bucket of water. Be a good neighbor. Try to leave the hot spring as clean as you found it. By doing this you will likely find the hot springs and the surrounding areas clean when you arrive.

### Camping at Hot Springs

You will be able to camp at some hot springs mentioned in this book which are located on public lands. If camping is not allowed, I will let you know.

### Equipment Needed

Well, you don't need much to have fun at most hot springs. Have bathing suits if you wish to bathe clothed at hot springs in the outback. Sometimes an old pair of tennis shoes or sandals will protect your feet from sharp rocks or pebbles. A bucket or pan for rinsing off will be helpful. Cold liquid refreshment will make your stay more pleasant. Be sure to bring towels. A rake will come in handy at some mucky hot springs. Lawn or beach chairs are handy. You can take a break from the hot water and sit in a nice chair and soak up the sun. Ultraviolet rays are much stronger in the High Sierra. So be careful not to be in the sun too long without a sun screen. Your skin can burn quite easily and quickly. You might want to wear a dry shirt or blouse while you're out of the pool.

It's a good idea to bring food with you even if you're only going to stay a short time. There won't be stores where you are going. You'll be surprised how hungry you get out in the wide open spaces and clean High Sierra air.

If you are going to camp, I suggest you at least have a tent to protect you from bugs seeking to suck your blood. You'll need sleeping bags, pillows, cooking and eating utensils, and a stove to cook on. Don't forget to have fuel for the stove. Oh, and matches and a can opener. What else? Make a written list and check items off as you put them in your vehicle.

### When Can Hot Springs Be Reached

Some hot springs at the higher elevations can only be reached in spring, summer and fall. If you are adventurous, others can be reached in winter with 4-wheel drive or by cross country skiing. I'll let you know about winter road conditions.

### Caution: Be Careful

Bathing in hot springs can be dangerous—even fatal, if you are not careful. Always, I repeat ALWAYS, test the water before stepping in. Hot springs can change temperature without notice. After all, the water bubbles up from the Earth and Nature is not always consistent. I will tell you about especially dangerous hot springs. You can test the water by very carefully sticking your finger in, or if you have a thermometer, by placing that in the water and checking the temperature.

Be sure to bring lots of liquid refreshment—and I don't mean just alcoholic beverages. Drinking too much alcohol and bathing in hot water can be lethal—especially for those with heart or respiratory problems.

Experts say bathing in water above 104 degrees Fahrenheit for long periods is not safe. Pregnant women should be cautioned about bathing in hot springs at all.

If you are taking a medication which can make you drowsy you should avoid bathing in hot springs. Falling asleep in a hot spring can be deadly. If possible, travel and bathe with another person. It is safer in case health problems arise. It's also a good idea to let others know where you are going and how long you will be there.

Be sure to drink lots of liquid while bathing in a hot spring. It is easy to dehydrate because you are unaware how much you are perspiring while in hot water.

It is not a good idea to jump or dive into hot springs. Older folks should be careful when getting in and out of the water.

Children should not be left by themselves at a hot spring. They should be warned not to jump or dive into the water. Be especially careful with younger children. They should not spend long periods in hot water.

Be careful and be safe. You'll have a better time.

Surprise Valley Hot Springs has private tubs right outside your room. You can control the water temperature yourself.

**Surprise Valley Hot Springs, Cedarville, CA**
**Location:** In extreme northeastern California about 5 miles east of Cedarville.
**Directions:** From Alturas drive north 6 miles on U.S. 395. Turn right, go east on CA 299, and drive 18 miles to Cedarville. When you come to the main drag in Cedarville, Surpise Valley Road, go straight, east 5 miles on Highway 299 to the gate of the resort. Turn right onto the road that leads 1/4 mile to the resort.
**Phone:** 1-877-927-6426; fax 1-530-279-6381
**Web site:** www.svhotsprings.com
**E mail:** warmh2o@hdo.net
**Seclusion:** Yes, perfect. Private spas just outside your room.
**Fee:** Hourly soaking $15 for 2 hours per person. Massage $39 for 30 minutes; $59 for one hour; $79 for one and a half hours.
**Open:** All year.
**Temperature:** Varies. You may control the temperature as you desire.

**One of the beautiful theme rooms at Surpise Valley Hot Springs. Each room is individually decorated. All rooms are warm and cozy with a door to the outside hot tub which is enclosed for privacy.**

**Condition:** A top of the line hot spring resort.

**Camping/Lodging:** Owners plan to have some RV spaces with full hook-ups beginning spring 2002. There are 10 rooms. Rates for standard lodging rooms week day are $85; weekend $95; deluxe rooms week day $105; weekend $115. No room telephones.

**George's 2 cents:** In the 1950's Curtis Rose's great grandfather bought a hot spring with a large outdoor pool in Surprise Valley outside of Cedarville. He enclosed the pool and built a lodge and motel rooms. In 1999 Curtis Rose and his wife Kim decided to restore the resort. They sold their home in Reno and invested in the resort. Today there are 10 lovely and cozy rooms each decorated with an individual theme and large private soaking tubs just outside the rooms. Both hot and cold water are piped into the tubs so you can control the temperature. The tub area is conrete with a wooden fence surrounding it for privacy. Underneath the concrete slab hot water is piped in to melt the snow in wenter. All the rooms are geothermally heated. All rooms have TV's, VCR's, kitchenettes and microwave.

There is a video library with over 500 videos free for guests. No phones, cable or satellite TV in rooms at this time. The Rose's will be opening a 5000 sq. ft conference center with dance floor in spring 2002. Fresh mineral water is piped in from an artesian spring 1 mile away. There are 3 artesian hot wells. The Rose's mix the fresh mineral water with the hot well water to cool the water. Customers may fly in to the small airport in Cedarville. The Rose's provide a courtesy car for private pilots to drive back and forth from the airport. Surprise Valley and the surrounding mountains are quiet and peaceful. This is great place to get away from the rat race with the one you love. Surprise Valley is one of the most geothermally active areas in California.

**One of the primitive soaking pools in the hot water ditch at Glen Hot Spring. The water flows from Glen Hot Spring ditch under the nearby road to Leondard Hot Spring. You will find a delapidated swimming pool at Leondard's.**

## Leonard Hot Spring, Cedarville, CA

**Location:** In extreme northeastern California about 6 miles northeast of Cedarville.
**Directions:** From Alturas drive north 6 miles on U.S. 395. Turn right, go east on CA 299, and drive 18 miles to Cedarville. In Cedarville, take a left, go north on the main drag, Surprise Valley Road, and drive 5.1 miles to 49 Lane. Turn right, go east, on 49 Lane 3.6 miles. About .8 miles out the road becomes a well graded gravel road. About 2.8 miles farther down the road you'll come to some corrals on your right. Drive about 400 yards till you come to the narrow creek that flows underneath 49 Lane. Park and follow the creek south.
**Seclusion:** Very good.
**Fee:** None.
**Open:** All year but you may need chains or four wheel drive in winter.
**Temperature:** About 150 degrees Fahrenheit at the source. Water cools the farther it flows down the creek. About a 105 degrees Fahrenheit at Leonard's.
**Condition:** Primitive.
**Camping:** Yes.
**George's 2 cents:** Hot water emerges from the base of barren foothills northeast of Cedarville. The source bubbles up from the ground in a slender ravine and it is too hot to bathe in. The water flows in a good size stream from the source through what is called Glen Hot Spring, then underneath 49 Lane, and then out through sagebrush and grasslands to Leonard Hot Spring. Actually Leonard's and Glen Hot Spring have the same source. However, someone years ago built a large swimming pool at Leonard's which has fallen apart and is no longer used. If you follow the stream as it leads from the road you can find some locally made tubs to soak. The stream is only about three feet wide. Water is about 105 degrees Fahrenheit. Plenty of room to camp and food, lodging and gas are available at Cedarville.

**The author points to the source for Glen and Leonard Hot Springs near Cedarville.**

### Glen Hot Spring, Cedarville, CA

**Location:** About 6 miles northeast of Cedarville.
**Directions:** Use the directions above for Leonard's Hot Spring. When you get to Leonard's, turn left on a dirt road that heads northeast and follows along the stream about a half mile to the source.
**Seclusion:** Very good.
**Fee:** None.
**Open:** All year.
**Temperature:** About 150 degrees Fahrenheit at the source.
**Condition:** Primitive.
**Camping:** Yes.
**George's 2 cents:** Locals have erected some primitive dams and a funky tub along the stream. The day I visited water in the main tub was about 118 degrees Fahrenheit, too hot for a soak. I went down stream and found a tub and took a soak. Lots of black goo on the

bottom but the water was great at about 105 degrees Fahrenheit. Both Glen and Leonard's lie in a narrow valley between dark, reddish mountains on the west and barren, light colored mountains on the east. The west part of the valley is green with alfalfa fields and trees. Ranchers raise cattle along the verdant strip that stretches along the western mountains. Cedarville is a funky little town off the beaten path well worth a visit for those who like small towns. Population is 800. There are a collection of businesses along Surprise Valley Road near Townsend. You'll find a car parts store, gas station, grocery store, restaurants and motels. Gerlach, Nevada is 87 miles southeast where there are other hot springs. See my book, *Hot Springs of Nevada* for more information.

**Eagleville Hot Spring, Eagleville, CA**
**Location:** About 23.8 miles south of Cedarville.
**Directions:** From the intersection of Surprise Valley Road and CA 299 in Cedarville, drive south 23.8 miles on Surprise Valley Road. 15.3 miles out you'll come to the tiny settlement of Eagleville. From the Eagleville General Store drive 8.5 miles south and look for a road on your left, east, going down the embankment.
**Seclusion:** Can be good to busy depending on the time of day and year.
**Fee:** None.
**Open:** All year.
**Temperature:** 115 degrees Fahrenheit at the source; 105 degrees F. in the wooden tub.
**Condition:** Clean and comfortable.
**Camping:** You could park beside the road I suppose.
**George's 2 cents:** Eagleville Hot Spring is right off the highway, and I mean right off the highway. You can park on the shoulder of the road and walk down the embankment to the hot spring. A steady source of hot water flows out of a pipe into a shallow pool. The water is also piped into a large wooden water tub, chest deep, just great for a soak. Locals have built wooden decking beside the tub which makes it easier to get in and out of the tub. I've soaked here twice and each time I had company, sooner or later. Last time, a trucker showed up soon after I arrived, then another trucker, then a car load of visitors. People know about the place, but Eagleville is so far out in

Top, taking a soak in the wooden tub at Eagleville, south of Cedarville. The water was just absolutely perfect temperature. Bottom, there is a shallow pool of warm water beside the tub at Eagleville Hot Spring where children can soak safely.

**The funky tub at Wild Mint Hot Spring just south of Eagleville Hot Spring.**

the sticks folks take real good care of the place. I did not see any trash when I last visited. Treat her right. One of the nicest hot springs I found in all northern California. When you're soaking in the tub, think of me.

**Wild Mint Hot Spring**
**Location:** About 1/4 mile south of Eagleville Hot Spring on the same side of the highway.
**Directions:** Drive 1/4 mile south from Eagleville Hot Spring. Look for an old abandoned cottage on the left. Park and walk down a path about 100 feet to the tub.
**Seclusion:** Good.
**Fee:** None.
**Open:** All year.
**Temperature:** 95 degrees Fahrenheit at the source.
**Condition:** Goofy.
**Camping:** Appears to be private land.
**George's 2 cents:** Wild Mint Hot Spring was named for the wild mint

**There are man made pools beside the Pit River at Big Bend where you can soak and adjust the temperature with river water.**

growing around the tub. Tub is easy to get to as its right off the highway. May be an alternative when Eagleville hot tub is busy.
One of three soaking tubs near the entrance of Big Bend Hot Springs

**Big Bend Hot Spring, Big Bend, CA**
**Location:** About 35 miles northeast of Redding, CA as the crow flies.
**Directions:** From Redding take CA 299 and drive northeast about 35 miles to Big Bend Road. Turn left, go north, on Big Bend Road 15.4 miles to the settlement of Big Bend, then turn left on Hot Spring Road. Drive .5 mile to the gate of Big Bend Hot Spring. Big Bend Road is about 16 miles west of the small town of Burney on CA 299.
**Phone:** 1(530-337-6606
**E mail:** rodj@299e.net
**Web site:** www.bigbendhotsprings.com
**Fee:** Day use $5 per person per day.
**Seclusion:** This is a public hot spring.
**Open:** All year.
**Temperature:** Varies at the different hot springs.

**One of the concrete soaking tubs at Big Bend Hot Springs.**

**Condition:** A lovely, funky resort in the forest beside the pleasant Pit River.

**Camping:** Yes. General camping is an extra $5 per day, an extra $10 for river edge camp sites.

**George's 2 cents:** It takes some trouble to get to Big Bend Hot Springs, but it's worth the drive. The resort is on 140 forested acres at the edge of the Pit River, a lovely clean river good for swimming and fishing. There are three concrete hot spring pools near the entrance to the resort. Other natural hot pools are located at the edge of the Pit River. To reach the pools by the river, drive 3/4 mile down the dirt road from the gate. Park your vehicle and follow a stone lined path 200 yards toward the river. You will find man made pools beside the  River. This is Indian Hot Springs. Water flows out of a hillside down through a garden of boulders to the pools beside the Pit River.The pools are formed by a circle of boulders. You can control the temperature of the water by the amount of river water you divert into the pools. Water entering the pools from Indian Springs is about 120 degrees Fahrenheit. I soaked in one of the pools

**Woody's Hot Spring is right beside the Feather River near Quincy.**

with temperature about 105 F.. The resort has apple trees, Concord grapes, black berries and reminds one of the Garden of Eden. Big Bend is a tiny settlement with a general store for basics. You can camp at the resort or at nearby Campgrounds. No gas station.

**Woody's Feather River Hot Spring, Quincy, CA**
**Location:** Just northwest of Quincy on the Feather River.
**Directions:** From the northern edge of Quincy drive north 10.1 miles on CA 70. At the intersection of CA 70 and 89, go west on CA 70, 4 miles to the resort. Park near the bar and walk 200 yards west on a path toward the river.
**Seclusion:** The place is right next to a highway and it is popular.
**Fee:** Owners ask for a small donation.
**Open:** All year. Closed each day from 10 p.m. to 7 a.m.
**Temperature:** About 95 degrees Fahrenheit.
**Condition:** One concrete tub, waist deep, for about 4-5 people.
**Camping:** Not at the hot spring but at nearby campgrounds.
**George's 2 cents:** The hot spring is located at the edge of the Feather River just down the embankment from CA 70. There is an RV park at

**The beautiful, sandy-bottomed tub at Sierraville Hot Springs made for a perfect soak on a warm October morning.**

the resort that was open when I visited. The Feather River is a lovely shallow river. There are lots of campgrounds in the area to camp. The bar and restaurant at Woody's are now closed.

**Sierra Hot Springs, Sierraville, CA**
**Phone:** (530) 994-3773
**Web site:** www.sierrahotsprings.com
**Location:** Just east of the town of Sierraville, north of Truckee.
**Directions:** From the intersection of I-80 and CA 89 in Truckee, drive north on CA 89, 21.9 miles to Sierraville. In Sierraville at the intersection of CA 89 and CA 49, turn right, go east on CA 49, .4 miles to Lemon Canyon Road. Turn right and drive .6 miles to Campbell Hot Spring Road and drive .8 mile to the resort.
**Seclusion:** There are private rooms and outdoor public bathing. Clothing is optional; most prefer bathing nude.
**Fee:** $10.00 for three hours; $15 for the whole day.
**Open:** All year.
**Temperature:** About 98 degrees Fahrenheit in the outdoor pool; 90

degrees Fahrenheit in the indoor tubs.

**Condition:** Good.

**Camping/Lodging:** Yes, in the campground. There are five lodging rooms at the hot spring and 10 at the nearby Globe Hotel. Rates range from $55-99.

**George's 2 cents:** The hot spring resort is run by the New Age Church of Being, the same folks who run Harbin Hot Springs at Middletown. ( See what I have to say about those folks under "Harbin Hot Springs." ) The staff has made considerable upgrades on the grounds. There are ten lodging rooms with a shared bath. Five indoor two person tubs are located above the lodge with a shower. A beautiful outdoor pool, with a sandy bottom and lovely landscaping is located about a quarter mile away. This is the one I preferred. The resort is located at the edge of a large alpine meadow. It's wonderful country. The restaurant is open on weekends. As is the case at Harbin, no drugs nor alcohol are allowed on the grounds. Eating meat is considered a no-no, but the boys chowdown on meat on two celebrations a year. Personally, I can do without the New Age nonsense. Though the staff claims to have no particular religious slant, there is a real push here for Eastern religions. The folks here have a sincere appreciation for Mother Earth, but seem to prefer worshipping the creations rather than the Creator. I confess I am politically incorrect. Sierraville is a sleepy town of 300 at an elevation of 4950 feet above sea level.


**Wilbur Hot Springs, west of Williams, CA**
**Phone** (530) 473-2306
**Web site:** www.wilburhotsprings.com
**Location:** Northwest of Sacramento about 60 miles as the crow flies.
**Directions:** From Sacramento, take I-5 about 60 miles to Williams. At Williams take the Highway 20 exit and go west about 18.6 miles to the intersection of Highway 20 and 16. Stay on Highway 20 and go about another 500 feet west of the intersection. Turn right onto Bear Valley Road. Drive 4 miles on a dirt road until you come to an old iron bridge. At the bridge turn left and follow the narrow road to a gate. Open the gate, drive through and shut the gate. It's about another mile to the resort.

**Wilbur Hot Springs with decks surrounding soaking pools.**

**Seclusion:** The place is out in the sticks but you will have company. People seem to prefer bathing nude. Clothing optional.

**Fee:** Day use $35  adult; $17.50 children. Must make reservations.

**Open:** All year. They don't want you to show up at the place before 10 AM. Use of the pools is between 10 AM and 5 PM for day use. Hot pools available 24 hours.

**Temperature:** Between 92-112 degrees Fahrenheit in the bath house. "Talking Tub" around 100 degree. There is a swimming pool with cold water in the summer.

**Condition:**  A clean, well kept resort in the sticks. Sauna and sun deck. 240 acres with  bike and hiking trails.

**Camping/Lodging:** Camping only in two tent camping spots. There is a hotel  with 19 private rooms, $140-160 per nite  and one private apartment  $158-225 per nite. There is bunk room where you can sleep communally with ten other strangers, $70 per person. Two camp sites at $47 per person per night. No phone service and no TV. The only power out here is solar power so they ask that you not bring electrical appliances. They  prefer  people  to call  first  before  just showing up. There is no restaurant or store to buy food so you must bring your own. There is a complete communal kitchen to cook in. Call for reservations and rate changes.

**George's 2 cents:** Of all the hot spring resorts I visited in northern California, my experience at Wilburs was the most bewildering. Some of the weird rules at Wilbur's are that you can't talk while using the bath house; it's the "quiet, meditative" place. However, there is the "Talking Tub" where you can actually talk to your friend or whomever you're with. I found a strange notice on a wall in the hotel which more or less said you should not laugh and have fun because your laughing might "intimidate" others who aren't having fun. The place gave me the creeps. It seems and to be infested with "New Agers" who have seen the light and pathetically and arrogantly look down on us "Old Agers" who believe God is still on the Throne where He belongs. I left Wilbur's thinking, what arrogance to tell people they can't talk or laugh when they are paying good money. The place is ridiculously over-priced and if you like the Darkness, you'll feel right at home. Carry a cross, silver bullets and a Bible wouldn't hurt either.

**Vichy Hot Springs, Ukiah, CA**
**Phone:** (707) 462-9515, fax (707 462-9515; E-mail vichy@pacific.net
**Web site:** www.vichysprings.com
**Location:** In northwestern California about 3 miles east of Ukiah.
**Directions:** From the San Francisco Bay area take Highway 101 north to Ukiah. Exit on Perkins-Vichy Springs Road. Turn right and drive 1.3 miles on Vichy Springs Rd. When you come to a T in the road where Vichy Springs Road meets Redemeyer Road, turn right and continue on Vichy Springs Road 1.7 miles to the resort. The drive from the bay area is about two hours.
**Seclusion:** This is a public resort.
**Fee:** All day rate is $35 per person or $22 per person for two hours or less.
**Open:** All year.
**Temperature:** 90 degrees Fahrenheit in the historic antique tubs. The water is heated to 104 degrees Fahrenheit in the Jacuzzi.
**Condition:** A beautiful resort with rooms and quaint cottages for lodging.

**Camping/Lodging:** No camping at the resort. Room rates are from $155 to $195. Cottages $255 per night; weekly rates available.Call for reservations and rate changes. Massages are $80 per hour.

**George's 2 cents:** Vichy Springs resort is easy to get to, about 3 miles off Highway 101. Frank Marble discovered the springs in 1848. In 1854 William Day established the first resort. Vichy's is one of the oldest continuously operating hot spring resorts in California. Writers Mark Twain, Robert Louis Stevenson and Jack London are said to have been visitors. Vichy Springs has a delightful bubbly, carbonated-alkaline water which first enters the antique tubs. Temperature in the tubs is about 90 degrees Fahrenheit and feels like a lukewarm bath. There are 4 outside antique soaking tubs; 6 inside soaking tubs. Curiously, the minerals in the carbonated water make you feel warmer the longer you stay in the tubs. There is a ten person sized Jacuzzi at about 104 degrees Fahrenheit and an Olympic size swimming pool in warm weather. There are nineteen individual rooms and 8 cottages for lodging with handicapped access; two conference rooms that can handle 200 people. The grounds are grassy with lots of shade trees. The resort is on 700 acres with hiking trails and a waterfall. Vichy's is a wonderfully quiet, civilized place to get away, but I'd call for reservations before coming. Massages and facials are available. The resort is currently owned and operated by Gilbert and Marjorie Ashoff, two of the most civilized persons you will ever meet; wonderful hosts. They put out a huge spread for Continental breakfast 7:30-10 a.m..The Asshoffs worked for nearly ten years to restore the resort, working tirelessly through the maze of Mendocino County red tape and regulations that would have stopped persons of lesser character. Their story alone is worth a novel.

Top, the antique soaking pools at Vichy Hot Springs. Below, the Jacuzzi is near the soaking pools for a quick hot dip.

Top, the Olympic size swimming pool at Vichy's. Below, the water fall above Vichy Springs that you can hike to.

**Outdoor soaking pools at Orr Hot Springs. There are indoor tubs also and a swimming pool to cool off.**

**Orr Hot Springs, Ukiah CA**
**Phone:** (707) 462-6277 Only answer the phone 12 noon to 8 p.m.
**Location:** About 14 miles northwest of Ukiah.
**Directions:** Heading north on Highway 101 take the North State Street exit in Ukiah. Turn right off the exit ramp and drive 1/4 mile on North State Street. Turn left onto Orr Springs Rd and drive 13 1/2 miles. It's about a two and a half hour drive from the Bay area.
**Seclusion:** There are private baths and areas for public bathing. People seem to prefer bathing nude. Clothing is optional.
**Fee:** Day use $19 per adult; $9.50 per child. Monday rates are $10 per adult; $6.50 per child. Call for current rates.
**Open:** All year. Call for reservations for day use and lodging.
**Temperature:** Ranges from 99 to 105 degrees Fahrenheit.
**Condition:** A laid-back, slightly funky resort in an isolated canyon in the mountains between Ukiah and Mendocino.
**Camping/Lodging:** Camping is $36 per adult; $20 per child. Room rates range from $36 to $145 on the weekends.

**George's 2 cents:** Leaving Ukiah on Orr Springs Rd you begin to climb up a very steep and winding road. Parts of the road there is a 10% grade. There are turns along this road that make a hair-pin curve seem like a freeway. I do not recommend RV's and trucks with trailers going up this road. Besides, when you get to the resort there is really no place to park an RV. The drive takes you through some wild country of golden wild oats, fennel, black berry bushes and stretches of dark pine forest. You climb for a long way and as you near the resort you begin a steep, twisting descent down the canyon to the resort. There are few houses and you feel like you are in the sticks. Toward the bottom of the canyon you reach the resort. You must park your car by the creek and walk a short ways to the resort. The resort is very quiet and solitude appears to be what some folks seek at Orr. There are several funky private rooms for personal bathing, an outside small soaking pool, an indoor redwood tub and a large swimming pool with cool water to zap yourself after a hot soak. A new steam room and sauna have been added.

History: The original bathhouse, now the dormitory for guests, was erected in the 1850's. This was when logging was a big industry in Mendocino County. Loggers bathed and socialized at the hot spring where there was a post office, saloon, dance hall and hotel (and I imagine a lot of booze.) The hotel burned down in the late 1930's and was replaced by a lodge and eight small cabins. The Wager family sold the springs to a group of Berkeley hippies in 1975 who turned the place into a commune and grew their own food. Today, Leslie Williams, the last of the original group, runs the place and is working hard to make lots of up-grades, including wheelchair access, doubling the size of the outdoor soaking area, two more private tubs and a steam room. Orr Hot Springs is in a dark, cozy heavily wooded canyon on 27 acres at the headwaters of the Big River. It is just a short distance from Montgomery Woods State Park where there are 1300 acres of forest with stands of old growth redwood trees. You are able to rent cabins, sleep in what is called a "Community room," or tent camp. Call for more details and reservations.

A couple enjoys a soak at Harbin Hot Springs near Middletown, California, north of Calistoga.

**Harbin Hot Springs, Middletown, CA**
**Phone:** In California call 1-800-622-2477. Outside California (707) 987-2477
**Web site:** www.harbin.org
**Location:** About 20 miles north as the crow flies from Calistoga.
**Directions:** From Calistoga, north of Santa Rosa, take CA 29 and drive north 17 miles to Middletown. In Middletown, turn left at the only stop light onto CA 175. Drive 3 blocks. Turn right onto Big Canyon Road. Drive 1.2 miles to you come to a Y in the road. Turn left onto Harbin Springs Road and drive 3 miles to the resort.
**Seclusion:** This is public bathing and clothing is optional.
**Fee:** Day use $20 per person; $25 per person on weekends.
**Open:** All year.
**Temperature:** Warm pool at 94 degrees Fahrenheit. Hot pool 112-118 degrees Fahrenheit. Cold plunge pool 50-60. Large swimming pool.
**Condition:** Recently renovated resort.
**Camping/Lodging:** Camping rates are $25-30 per person per day.

RV 's less than 20 ft. camp at the same rate. No hookups. Lodging in 40 rooms from dormitory rooms at $35 to regular rooms at $220 per night.

**George's 2 cents:** Well, if you wondered where the whacked-out hippies from the 60's and 70's went, they moved to Harbin Hot Springs. The place is operated by New Agers who are into Yoga and Zen. "You know man, life is a circle, a never ending circle, and you are the key to the universe" etc., etc.. Actually, the New Agers are simply humanists, humanism now being an Old Idea, that being, Man is his own salvation. Right. Let us take a moment to review the history of mankind. The last time I ran into these folks was back in the late 60's. I thought they had all moved to Mars. Please forgive me, I am totally politically incorrect.

There are rules at this place for nearly everything, except one: You can walk around naked and nobody will arrest you. If you don't have a registration ticket on your windshield, they'll lock up your wheels with a device that will cost you $25 to get unhitched. The day I arrived the folks were having their yearly Pagan Festival and the grounds were loaded with everything from tree worshippers to Satanists. (Personally, anyone who wants to carve out *my* heart and roast *my* butt on a fire to make a few points with their pal the Devil, is not my friend.) You can't drink or smoke on the grounds. And they are all vegetarians, so if you want some real food, you must drive back to Middletown. ( Personally I have a bumper sticker on my truck that reads thus: I EAT VEGETARIANS. ) The boys have a Health food store, and a couple cafes that serve—you guessed it—rabbit food, and community kitchen where you can cook your own food. However, if you fry up some bacon or a rib eye steak, you'll likely be asked to hit the trail. These guys appear to take their occult ideas totally serious and they expect you to as well. And if you don't, well, there's something wrong with you. And like other hot springs resorts run by the occult, oh, they love their silence. The place gave me the creeps. There's an outdoor swimming pool, indoor hot tub, outdoor tubs, and lots of room for lying around naked. 1400 acres of hiking trails. Carry your cross and silver bullets.

## Calistoga Hot Springs

"...the whole neighborhood of Mt. St. Helena is full of sulphur and boiling springs...and Calistoga itself seems to repose on a mere film above a boiling, subterranean lake."
*Robert Louis Stevenson*

A huge subterranean aquifer of hot water resides beneath the little town of Calistoga north of Santa Rosa. Industrious entrepreneurs have drilled wells into the aquifer and piped the hot water into various resorts throughout Calistoga. Just outside of town there is The Old Faithful Geyser which erupts with hot water about every forty minutes.

## Golden Haven Hot Springs
**Phone:** (707) 942-6793
**Web site:** www.glenhaven.com
**Location:** 1713 Lake Street.
**Directions:** Coming in from the south, take Lincoln, the main drag, to Grant, turn left and then right on Lake Street.
**Seclusion:** This is a public place. Clothing required.
**Fee:** None if you rent a room.
**Open:** All year.
**Temperature:** A large indoor swimming pool at around 95 degrees Fahrenheit. A Jacuzzi at around 104 degrees Fahrenheit.
**Condition:** Good. Air conditioned rooms with TV and fridge. Some rooms have two bedrooms and a kitchenette. No phones in rooms.
**Camping/Lodging:** No camping, just motel rooms. Rates range from $65 to $175.
**George's 2 cents:** This is where I stayed in Calistoga. Glen Haven is off the main drag and there are shade trees which is vital during the summer. Calistoga is hotter than the Dickens in summer and early autumn. Above the indoor pool there is a place to sun bathe with lawn chairs. There's a place to barbecue out of doors. Rooms have cable TV without remote and a fridge which will be appreciated in summer. Massage and treatments are available. No room phones at this writing.

**Golden Haven's indoor warm pool with Jacuzzi in the rear.**

**Calistoga Village Inn and Spa**
**Phone:** (707) 942-0991
**Web Site:** www.greatspa.com
**Location:** 1880 Lincoln Avenue, at the far north end of town.
**Directions:** Go north on the main drag, Lincoln Avenue to 1880 Lincoln. It's on the right side.
**Seclusion:** This is a public place. Clothing required.
**Fee:** None when you rent a room. Day use for mineral baths is $35 for a 30 minute bath.
**Open:** All year.
**Temperature:** 85-104 degrees Fahrenheit. Three mineral pools, sauna and jacuzzi.
**Condition:** Excellent.
**Camping/Lodging:** No camping. Room rates are $69-159 per night all year.
**George's 2 cents:** Lodging is in typical motel rooms with two person private Jacuzzi. The resort specializes in various treatments, mineral baths, mud baths, massage, salt scrub, mini facial and mustard bath.

**This is what you're in for with a Calistoga mud bath.**

Call for current rates. 10% discount on treatments for lodging guests. There's a restaurant next door for convenience open between 5-9 PM and closed on Mondays.

**Indian Springs**
**Phone:** (707) 942-4913; fax 707-942-4919
**Web site:** www.IndianSpringsCalistoga.com
**Location:** 1712 Lincoln Avenue.
**Directions:** Go east and then north on the main drag to 1712 Lincoln Avenue. The resort is on the right side.
**Seclusion:** This is a public place. Private treatments are available.
**Fee:** None for guests. Day use is $20 for adults; $10 for children under 13.
**Open:** All year.
**Temperature:** Temperature in the large public swimming pool is kept between 90-102 degrees Fahrenheit depending on the season. There is an Olympic sized swimming pool with water between 90-102 degrees Fahrenheit depending on the time of the

The Olympic size warm pool at Indian Springs.

year.

**Condition:** Excellent.

**Camping/Lodging:** No camping. Rooms are in 15 bungalow duplexes with kitchenettes with full size fridges, micro waves, coffee makers and toasters. Two bungalows are small separate houses with full kitchens and cooking stoves. Bungalows range in size from one to three bedrooms. Current rates range from $185-$500 per night year round. Check in time is 3 PM. No pets. Two complimentary mud baths with weeknight stays Sunday thru Thursday, November 1-March 31. Reservations are recommended. Summer season is the busiest time.

**George's 2 cents:** Sam Brannan, the first Gold Rush millionaire, bought the hot spring and the grounds in 1860 and built the first resort. He named the site "Calistoga" by combining the names of California with Saratoga. Leland Stanford purchased the property in the 1880's and for a time considered using it as the site for Stanford University.

**Doc Wilkinson's indoor Jacuzzi. There are outdoor pools too.**

The resort is located on perhaps the largest resort grounds in Calistoga. There is an Olympic sized swimming pool with water between 90-102 degrees Fahrenheit depending on the time of the year. Around the pool you will find a billiards table, ping pong table, chess and checker games. Nearby is a lovely grassy lounging area and a playground for kids. You can also rent three wheel surrey bicycles to peddle around town.

The bungalows were built in the 1940's, renovated in 1988. The bungalows have plank floors, white washed walls, fireplaces, color TV's, air conditioning, down comforters, terry cloth robes and hammocks outside each bungalow.

The resort does not have a hot tub nor Jacuzzi. Indian Springs instead specializes in 15 different massage treatments and mud baths. These consist of tubs full of volcanic ash mud which is heated with piped in mineral water. The baths are said to remove impurities from the body and improve circulation. The resort also has mineral baths, steam room, blanket wrap and you can be served with citrus and cucumber drinks while boiling yourself in the mud baths.

**Dr. Wilkinson's Hot Springs Resort**
**Phone:** (707) 942-4102
**Web site:** www.drwilkinson.com
**Location:** 1507 Lincoln Avenue.
**Directions:** The resort is right in the middle of town on the main drag.
**Seclusion:** This is a public place. Private therapies are available.
**Fee:** $149 for day use with one hour body massage; Salon Facial and Cerofango Treatment for hands and feet.
**Open:** All year.
**Temperature:** 102-04 degrees Fahrenheit in the indoor Jacuzzi; 80 degrees Fahrenheit in one outdoor warm pool; 75 degrees Fahrenheit in swimming pool.
**Condition:** Excellent.
**Camping/Lodging:** $109-189 per night. All rooms have color TV, drip coffee makers, telephones and air conditioning. Call for reservations and rate changes.
**George's 2 cents:** Dr. Wilkinson is a chiropractor who came to Calistoga in 1946. He's pretty much retired now but does some therapies. Other masseuses nowadays cover for the doc. There are all sorts of treatments from facials to massages to mud baths. Separate bungalows are available. No pets.

**Roman Spa Hot Springs Resort**
**Phone:** 1 (800) 404-4772 or (707) 942-4441
**Location:** 1300 Washington Street.
**Directions:** Heading into town from the south on CA 29, take a left on Washington Street and drive one block.
**Seclusion:** This is a public place. Private rooms and treatments are available.
**Fee:** Varies for various treatments.
**Open:** All year.
**Temperature:** Large outdoor pool 92-95 degrees Fahrenheit; indoor hydrojet therapy pool 100 degrees Fahrenheit; outdoor hydrojet therapy pool 105 degrees Fahrenheit.
**Condition:** A beautiful, top of the line spa with gorgeous rooms.
**Camping/Lodging:** No camping. Rooms range from $125 to $239 per night. The high season is July and August. Reservations recommended. Call for reservations and rate changes.

**The outdoor pool at Roman Spa Hot Springs Resort.**

**George's 2 cents:** What I first noticed was the lovely landscaping of plants and flowers around the pool area and grounds. Very well kept up. Large outdoor pool area with inside and outdoor pools and sunbathing area. The lodging rooms are beautifully accommodated. Massage treatments available.

**Eurospa and Inn**
**Phone:** (707) 942-6829; fax (707) 942-1138
**Web site:** www.eurospa.com
**Location:** 1202 Pine Street.
**Directions:** Heading into town from the south on CA 29, take a right on Cedar Street and drive two blocks.
**Seclusion:** This is a public place. Private rooms and treatments are available.
**Fee:** Varies for various treatments.
**Open:** All year.
**Temperature:** Outdoor pool 92-95 degrees Fahrenheit; outdoor Jacuzzi pool 105 degrees Fahrenheit.

**Outdoor pool and Jacuzzi at Eurospa and Inn.**

**Condition:** A quiet back street motel with outdoor pool and Jacuzzi.
**Camping/Lodging:** No camping. Rooms range from $75-229.
**George's 2 cents:** Eurospa is a quiet place off the main drag. Pool area is surrounded by grass for a good place to sunbathe. "Peter" the pool keeper, takes extra special care of the pool and works very hard to keep the pool and waters very clean. Peter took time to explain to me that the water must be treated with 1.5 parts chlorine per million to keep the water just right.

**Calistoga Spa Hot Springs**
**Phone:** (707) 942-6269
**Web site:** www.calistogaspa.com
**Location:** 1006 Washington Street.
**Directions:** Heading into town from the south on CA 29, take a right on Washington Street and drive two blocks.
**Seclusion:** This is a public place. Private rooms and treatments are available.
**Fee:** Mineral pools are open to the public. Weekday use fee is $10 per

person including children one year old and older; weekend fee $15 per person.

**Open:** All year.

**Temperature:** There are four pools of varying sizes ranging in temperatures from 83 to 105 degrees Fahrenheit.

**Condition:** Excellent. Perhaps the largest spa in Calistoga with a huge pool area with four pools and large sunbathing area. Conference room and exercise room available.

**Camping/Lodging:** No camping. Rooms range from $121-176. High season is from March to October. Weekend rates are higher. Call for reservations and rate changes.

**George's 2 cents:** Perhaps the busiest spa I found in Calistoga. The pool area was loaded with people the morning I visited. Massages and therapies available as in the other Calistoga spas. Good size exercising room with top of the line equipment. Large parking lot for RV's.

**Nances Hot Springs**

**Phone:** (707) 942-6211

**Web site:** www.nanceshotsprings.com

**Location:** 1614 Lincoln Avenue.

**Directions:** Heading into town from the south on CA 29, head to the north end of town. Nances is on the right hand side of the street.

**Seclusion:** This is a public place. Private treatments are available.

**Fee:** Day use $20 per day weekdays only.

**Open:** All year.

**Temperature:** 102-104 degrees Fahrenheit.

**Condition:** A hotel with twenty-four rooms and one indoor small soaking pool.

**Camping/Lodging:** No camping. 24 lodging rooms, some with twin beds. All rooms have kitchenettes. Rooms rates $65 for a single weekdays; $72 double on the weekdays; $115-125 weekends. Reservations are recommended. Call for rate changes. Senior 10% discount Sunday-Thursday.

**George's 2 cents:** Nances is one of the most reasonable Calistoga spas. There is one indoor pool for soaking. Nances has the regular massage treatments and mud baths available at other Calistoga spas. One of the features I liked best are the kitchenettes in each room for those who want to stay in town a while and cook for themselves. Located right in town so everything is in walking distance.

**Sonoma Mission Inn and Sp, a, Boyesot Springs, CA**
**Phone:** (707) 938-9000; 1 (800) 862-4945
**Location:** In the heart of Boyes Hot Springs just north of Sonoma.
**Directions:** From Napa, take CA 12/121 west 11 miles to the intersection of CA 12 and CA 121. Go north on CA 12, 4 miles to Sonoma. Keep heading north 3 miles to Boyes Blvd. Turn left and you're there.
**Seclusion:** This is a public place. Private rooms and treatments are available.
**Fees:** Would not provide prices.
**Open:** All year.
**Temperature:** Outdoor exercise pool 82 degrees Fahrenheit; outdoor spa pool 90 degrees Fahrenheit; 102 degrees F. in the outdoor whirlpool. There is a single whirlpool in the indoor spa.
**Condition:** A top of the line, gorgeous Four Star hotel.
**Camping/Lodging:** No camping. Rooms rates from $189-1,000. Reservations are recommended.
**George's 2 cents:** History: H.E. Boyes struck hot mineral water in 1895 while drilling a well. He built a bathhouse, and five years later a hotel. In 1923 a fire completely destroyed the town of Boyes Hot Springs and the hotel. The current hotel was built in 1927 as a replica of a California Mission. In 1991 a new well was drilled 1,000 feet where the mineral water registered 135 degrees Fahrenheit. The mineral water is piped into pools and whirlpools. The hotel is beautiful with all sorts of activities, massages and treatments and there is a tennis court. Day use for non-registered guests is Monday-Friday only. Some hotel rooms have fireplaces.

**White Sulphur Springs Resort and Spa. St. Helena, CA**
**Phone:** 1(800) 593-8873; (707) 963-8588; fax (707) 963-2890;
**Web site:** www.whitesulphursprings. com
**Location:** 3 miles west of the heart of St. Helena in the Napa Valley.
**Directions:** From CA 29 heading into and out of St. Helena north and south, go west on Spring Street to White Sulphur Springs Rd. It's 3 miles from the Intersection of CA 29 and Springs Rd to the resort.

**The triangular warm pool at White Sulphur Springs at St. Helena.**

**Seclusion:** This is a public place. Private rooms and treatments are available.
**Fee:** Day use $30 for non-registered guests. Free to guests.
**Open:** All year.
**Temperature:** Outdoor pool is not heated; temperatures in the outdoor pool vary with the weather. Outdoor Jacuzzi for 20 people 104 degrees Fahrenheit; outdoor triangular shaped sulphur spring pool directly from the spring 85-92 Fahrenheit.
**Condition:** A nicely restored resort with green grass, landscaping on 330 acres.
**Camping/Lodging:** No camping. 37 rooms which include 9 creekside cottages. Room rates $85-205.
**George's 2 cents:** The resort is nestled in a canyon west of St. Helena amongst Redwood, Madrone and Fir trees. There is a large outdoor swimming pool, Jacuzzi that fits about 20 people and an outdoor triangular spring fed pool. The spa has all sorts of treatments like mud wraps, but no mud baths. It's close to town for restaurants, and yet far enough away for those who are looking for a quiet, green place to recoup. Good place for group meetings, weddings etc.. Lots

**The outdoor Jacuzzi at White Sulphur Springs resort, St. Helena.**

of room to take hikes and listen to the birds.

**Grover Hot Springs State Park**
**Phone:** (530) 694-2248
**Location:** 4 miles west of Markleeville, California.
**Directions:** From Minden, Nevada drive 16 miles south on Highway 88. At Woodford's turn left and drive 7 miles to Markleeville. In Markleeville follow the road signs 4 miles to Grover Hot Springs State Park.
**Open:** All year. Summer hours 9 a.m. to 9 p.m. daily. Winter hours 9 a.m.-9 p.m. Saturday and Sunday 2 p.m.-9 p.m. Monday-Friday.
**Seclusion:** This is a public place.
**Fee:** $1 per child per entry. Adults $2. Call for current rates.
**Temperature:** Two pools; one at 70-80 degrees Fahrenheit, the other at 102-105.
**Condition:** Good. This is a public resort. There's a campground with outdoor pools, showers and rest rooms.

**Grover's Hot Spring pool on a chilly spring afternoon.**

**Camping:** Yes, 76 camp sites. $12 per night for 8 persons and 2 vehicles. YOU MUST MAKE RESERVATIONS TO CAMP. You can make reservations 2 days to 7 months in advance. To make reservations call 1-800-444-7275 .

**George's 2 cents:** Grover's is highly visited during the summer. If you like being around people, you'll like Grover's. There are lots of hiking trails and streams for trout fishing. It's a nice place for the family. If you want to camp, call to reserve a site. The hot pools are on a first come, first served basis. Capacity is 50 and this number is reached early on summer days. Every time your kid leaves the pool area and wants to return to the pool, they must pay $1.

**East Carson River Hot Spring #1**

**Location:** Located on the west side of the East Carson River approximately 6 miles northeast of Markleeville, California and 12 miles south of Gardnerville, Nevada. It is located 9.8 miles down a dirt road southwest of U.S. Highway 395, very near the California/Nevada

**This small stream is the source for East Carson Hot Spring#1.**

border.

**Directions:** There are two ways to the hot spring: by road and by river. The way by road now may not be possible, as I understand the owner of the ranch near the hot spring will no longer allow persons to cross his property to the hot spring. That means the only other way is by raft down the East Carson River from Markleeville, California.

Road directions: From Raley's Supermarket in Gardnerville, Nevada, drive 11.9 miles south on U.S. 395 to Leviathan Mine Road. This road will be on your right, or west, and there will be a valley on the right side of the highway where you turn onto the road. Drive west on Leviathan Mine Road 1.8 miles until you come to U.S. Forest Service road 189. This road should be marked. Forest Service road 189 branches off Leviathan Mine Road to your right. This becomes a much narrower road.

2.6 miles down the canyon you will reach Doud Spring on your left. .6 miles further you will cross the creek on a very narrow bridge. .5 miles on and you will reach an overlook and see the Carson River on your right. .1 mile further the road forks; go straight. You will

**Hot water tumbles over an embankment into a man made pool beside the East Carson River. There is a second hot spring about a quarter mile up river on the same side of the river.**

come to the steel gate at the River Ranch. This is private property. The past owner generally granted permission to cross the ranch to the hot springs. If this gate is closed, or posted with a "No Trespassing" sign, you cannot go further.

2 miles from here you come to a narrow wooden bridge across a ditch. Cross carefully. 2.2 miles further and you reach the Carson River. Forest Service road 189 literally ends at the river's edge. In fall you can cross the river in a 4-wheel drive vehicle carefully to the west side of the river. Or cross the river on foot.

Directions by River: You can raft down the East Carson River from Markleeville about 10 miles to the hot spring. Contact Bob Rudden at the Markleeville General Store **1-530-694-2448**. Bob and Dee Rudden provide a service where they will drive your vehicle down the river so you can meet your vehicle after your river raft trip. There is a fee, of course.

**Seclusion:** Although this hot spring is 9.8 miles off the highway, it is a popular place. Best times to visit will be in the early spring and autumn during the week, early mornings and early evenings.

**Temperature:** About 104 degrees Fahrenheit.

**Condition:** A nice primitive pool with rock sides and a sandy bottom; it is built beside the river.

**Fee:** None.

**Camping:** Yes.

**George's 2 cents:** The author of another popular hot spring guide writes that the only way to this spring is by raft down the East Carson River. Wrong. He also says the springs do not appear on any U.S. Government map. Wrong again. These springs appear on the Toiyabe National Forest map, Carson District and on the U.S.G.S. map Carters Station Quadrangle. This information comes from the same author who tells you the approximate location of hot springs but often does not give directions. And people buy his book.

Those who have ridden the road to Hell, that is, the road to Saline Valley, ( *See* my book, *Hot Springs of the Eastern Sierra* ) can now have the experience of riding the road to Purgatory. Leviathan Mine Road for the mere 1.8 miles you drive it, is a freeway compared to U.S. Forest Service road 189. This road leads down a narrow canyon beside Bryant Creek. The road is terribly rocky. I do not advise anyone to make the trip in an RV or standard automobile. There are several places where there are tight, deep ditches where you will need all the bottom clearance God will grant you. Your tires should be in good shape and be certain you've got a good spare tire. Although the road from Highway 395 is a mere 9.8 miles it seems like a hundred. It took me a good forty-five minutes to make the drive and I had been over most of the road the preceding spring. When you reach the bottom of the canyon you will come to River Ranch, complete with posts and barbed-wire and a few cattle gates.CLOSE THE GATES when you've passed through.

This is private property; the former owner allowed folks to pass through the ranch to the hot springs. I have information that the new owner does not. They plant cattle out in the meadows in late spring until around November 15. From the steel gate at River Ranch it is still 3.2 miles to the hot springs. The dirt road leads east and around the ranch. It may seem like you are going away from the river, and you are. But it is necessary in order to avoid the meadows which are muddy and treacherous most of the year. Signs along the way tell you to stay out of the meadows, so STAY OUT OF THE MEADOWS.

There are several very steep stretches toward the end of the ride. I shifted into 4-wheel drive at these spots and made it just fine.

The road will dead-end at the east fork of the Carson River. The East Carson River Hot Spring #1 is located right across the river on the west side. There are currently two outhouses, one on each side of the river. The hot springs and the Carson River are a real nice places to visit and tent camp. There are some fine pools for fly fishing. Keep in mind you are in California, so you will need a California fishing license although you began your trip from Nevada.

There used to be a way to the hot springs from Markleeville down a jeep trail called Cottonwood Canyon. However, this road crosses private property. I understand the current owners no longer allow people to cross their property to the springs.

In the spring time, the road through River Ranch can be mucky and treacherous. I would not advise going over this road until it dries in late spring. Even then, there will be a few mucky spots.

If the gate at the ranch is locked or posted No Trespassing, the only way to reach the hot spring is by river from Markleeville.

**East Carson River Hot Spring #2**
**Location:** Located on the east side of the East Carson River 100 yards up river from East Carson River Hot Spring #1.
**Directions:** Cross the East Carson River at the East Carson River Hot Spring. The river bottom has small, smooth stones and in late summer and autumn the depth is about a foot. A dirt road across the river heads east. Take this toward the river. The road forks. Go left and follow the rocky road down to the Carson River. The hot springs are located approximately 100 yards on the east side of Carson River.
**Seclusion:** Excellent.
**Temperature:** Approximately 100 degrees Fahrenheit where you bathe.
**Condition:** A stream of water drops about twenty feet down into a knee deep primitive pool.
**Fee:** None.
**Camping:** Yes. You are on U.S. Forest Service land.

**Fales Hot Spring Ditch is right next to the highway about 13 miles north of Bridgeport. The ditch has several waist deep pools.**

**George 2 cents:** Once again the author of another hot spring guide is wrong. He says this hot spring is located *down* river from East Carson River Hot Spring. It is actually located up river.

**Fales Hot Spring Ditch**
**Location:**  13 miles north of Bridgeport on U.S. Highway 395.
**Directions:**  From Bridgeport, take U.S. Highway 395, and drive 13 miles north. You will find the closed resort on your left. Drive .3 miles north and park in a small gravel turnout. The hot spring ditch is to your right just down the embankment.
**Seclusion:**  You're right next to a highway.
**Fee:** No.
**Temperature:**  The source is extraordinarily hot but cools as it flows down the ditch. When I last soaked in the ditch the water was 92 degrees Fahrenheit, just perfect.
**Condition:**  A narrow ditch with hot water with several large pools

**A boy takes a swim in the large warm pool at Big Hot Spring just south of Bridgeport.**

made by damning the ditch.

**Camping:** No, but nearby there is plenty of public land for camping.

**George's 2 cents:** Well, here's the story. Sam Fales built a resort here back in the 1880's. However, the resort has been closed for years. You can't use the water on the west side of the highway because it's on private property. The ditch however on the east side of the highway appears to be on U.S. Forest Service land.

**Bridgeport Hot Springs**

**Big Hot**

**Location:**  About 2 miles southeast of Bridgeport, California.

**Directions:** 1.5 miles south of Bridgeport, you will find a gate on the east side of the highway. You must park here and walk about 1 mile east to the white knoll where the pool is located.

**Accessibility:** All year.

**Seclusion:** Depending on the time of day, you can have the hot springs to yourselves. I would suggest mornings before 10, evenings around 5.

**Fee:** None.

**Temperature:** Approximately 95 degrees Fahrenheit.

**Condition:** There are six pools, but the largest, called Big Hot is the most often used. This is a natural rock warm pool and it is deep. Children should wear life jackets and always be attended. There are rock ledges around the sides of the pool to help you get in and out.

**Camping:** No.

**George 2 cents:** Here's the New story: Big Hot was available for the whole Bridgeport community to use for decades until new owners purchased the property several years ago to "protect it" as I was told. However, one owner admitted to me they had bought the spring for their personal use. They then fenced the property so people could no longer drive to Big Hot. This did not make people in the community happy, especially since the new owners lived far away. One owner informed me that the new owners will only allow persons to hike to the hot spring. Where you could drive to the spring for decades, you can no longer do so. You must park your car along the highway. If the owners should post No Trespassing signs, **then you are on notice you can not enter the property.** This once was one of my very favorite hot springs. It was easy to reach right off the highway. Often you had the place to yourself. For centuries the Paiutes camped, bathed and lived beside this pool. This is a wonderful place. Please keep it clean and safe. Take out what you bring in. It is a terrible shame to see what has happened to this wonderful place.

**Travertine Hot Spring**

**Location:** 1 mile southeast of Bridgeport.

**Directions:** Head south from Bridgeport on U.S. Highway 395, .5 miles to Jack Sawyer Road. Turn left and drive .3 miles, then turn left onto a dirt road and follow it 1.3 miles up, then down, then up a hill. Portions of this road are quite rutted. Stay on the main road. I made it in with my trailer but I had to be careful. You will come up a hill and there will be a long ridge of travertine, rock, on your right. Turn right here and follow the road on the east side of the rock ridge.

**Accessibility:** You will need 4-wheel drive in winter or you can

Top, taking a soak in the concrete pool at Travertine Hot Spring near Bridgeport. Bottom, man made pools at the south end of the Travertine Hot Spring area. Water gracefully tumbles down from a mound of Travertine.

## Bridgeport Hot Springs

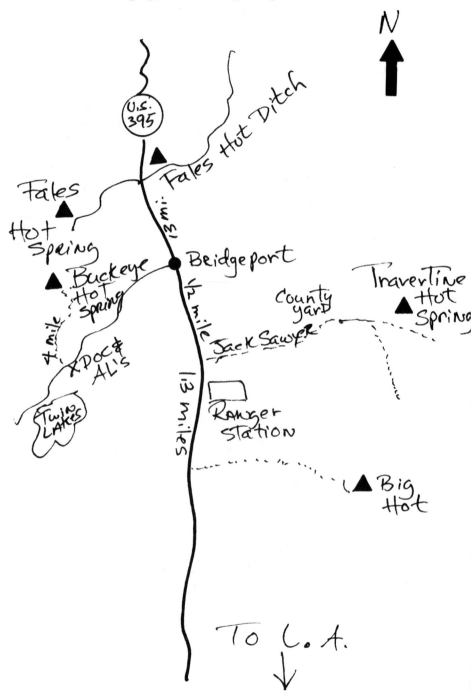

cross-country ski in.

**Seclusion:** This is a popular hot spring. Best times for bathing alone will be early in the morning or late at night. Even then you may have company.

**Fee:** None

**Temperature:** 95-105 degrees.

**Condition:** There are several tubs in the area. The original tubs are located below Travertine bluffs where the water tumbles down from Travertine Bluff. The primitive man made tubs have clay bottoms. Very enjoyable. However, there is another new tub made of concrete, Jacuzzi size, with a drain and carpet surrounding the tub. This is now the most popular tub.

**Camping:** Not anymore. BLM stopped camping about six years ago. Why? People were having fun and not bothering anyone. Angry that the BLM has restricted use of *your* public lands? Call the BLM at (760) 872-4881 and ask them why you can't camp on your federal lands when cows can.

**George 2 cents:** This is a nicely developed hot spring. And quite interesting, too. A spring emerges at the crest of a ridge at Travertine Bluff. A cut along the ridge carries the water to four hot spring pools located below. One, is large enough for one person and is very hot. Two are about the size of Jacuzzi and the water is around 95 degrees Fahrenheit. The third pool is a smaller pool and cooler.

Recent earthquakes for a time caused the hot spring on Travertine Bluff not to flow, or drastically reduced the flow. The flow has recently increased, but it is still not the same.

This is a popular spot. I enjoy these hot springs but if you're looking for privacy, this may not be the spot spring and summer. BLM provides a portable toilet spring and summer. Please do not dump trash in the toilet or we will lose it. And you girls know what that means.

**Buckeye Hot Spring**

**Location:** About 5 miles west of Bridgeport near Buckeye camp - ground.

**Directions:** From Bridgeport take Twin Lakes road 7.1 miles to Doc and Al's Campground. Turn right here and follow the dirt road 4

**Looking down on Buckeye Creek Hot Spring just west of Bridge-
port. Buckeye is a very popular place in summer.**

miles toward Buckeye Campground. Just past a one lane bridge, the
road forks. Take the second dirt road on your right and follow it up
the hill .4 miles. You'll find a parking area on your right. Park here
and walk down a steep trail toward the creek and the hot spring.
**Seclusion:** It's visited often in the spring and summer.
**Accessibility:** You'll need 4-wheel drive in winter and even then it
may be impossible.
**Fee:** None for the hot spring.
**Temperature:** About 105 degrees Fahrenheit. Hot but comfortable.
Temperature can be controlled by a pipe that brings cold water in
from the river.
**Condition:** This is a nice, clear and clean hot spring pool. A rock dam
holds the water to make a pool.
**Camping:** Not at the hot spring but at the campground.
**George 2 cents:** Hot spring water emerges from a hillside at the
bottom of the canyon beside Buckeye Creek. Locals have made a pool

out of river rock beside the creek. You can cool the pool by letting in more creek water. Buckeye's is one of the more popular hot springs in the area, especially amongst those who prefer bathing nude. More private in mornings. If you're looking for privacy in spring and summer, this is not the spot. If it has been a good winter, spring run off may destroy the rock pools and they must be rebuilt. Camping is nearby.

## Mono Lake Hot Springs
There are hot springs on the south and north shores of Mono Lake.

## Dechambeau Ranch Hot Spring Ponds
**Location:** On the north shore of Mono Lake northeast of Black Point.
**Directions:** From Lee Vining, drive south on U.S. 395 6.8 miles to the intersection of U.S. 395 and CA 167. Turn right on to CA 167 and drive east 4.5 miles to Cemetery Road. Turn right on Cemetery Road and drive south 1 mile. You'll find a dirt road to your left. Turn left and follow the dirt road along the fence .8 miles to the Ponds parking lot. Pass through the gate and walk about 100 yards northeast on a dirt path, then turn right and follow a path about 200 yards to the ponds.
**Seclusion:** Yes, plenty.
**Fee:** None.
**Temperature:** Hot enough to burn you at the source. Cooler in the ponds the farther you get away from the source.
**Condition:** Primitive.
**Camping:** No.
**George's 2 cents:** Well, this is not a hot spring that appeals to me. The hot spring ponds are now part of the Mono Basin National Forest Service Area. Here's the story: long ago they were drilling for oil out here. They didn't hit oil but struck extremely hot water. Keep in mind this is a highly volcanic area. Anyway, they piped the water into a concrete tub that was supposedly used to scald pigs. Hot water emerges from a pipe into the ponds. **THE WATER IS SCALDING HOT. DO NOT TOUCH.** Ranch buildings still stand nearby which you can visit but not enter. Nice quiet place for a picnic. Two wheel drive vehicles should stay on the main road and not go into the pumice sand. If you do, you have a 99% chance of getting stuck in the

Dechambeau Ponds is now part of a cooperative protective venture between the U.S. Forest Service and other agencies. Interesting place to visit. You may picnic at the nearby ranch.

sand, and well, there you are, stuck and a long way from help. Stay on the main roads out here. Even then be careful.

**Navy Beach Hot Spring**
**Location:** 11 miles southeast of Lee Vining.
**Directions:** From Lee Vining, take U.S. Highway 395, 5.2 miles south to Highway 120. Take Highway 120 east 4 miles until you reach a road sign, "Tufa Reserve." Turn left, north, down a dirt road toward Mono Lake. The road forks. Take the Navy Beach road. It goes to the right. You'll come to another dirt road that goes east and west. Turn left, and follow the road a half mile to the Navy Beach parking area. Take the path on the west side of the parking lot 1/4 mile to the hot spring.
**Seclusion:** Best times for privacy are in the early morning and at night. Best seasons for private visits are spring and fall.

**Navy Beach Hot Spring on the southern shore of Mono Lake.**

**Fee:** None
**Temperature:** 95 degrees Fahrenheit.
**Condition:** Primitive.  About the size of a large Jacuzzi. There are hidden rocks in the pool. **DO NOT DIVE OR JUMP IN.** By the way, the water contains arsenic. Do not drink it.
**Camping:** Not permitted.
**George's 2 cents:** With the increase of water into Mono Lake, the level of the Lake has risen and the hot spring is now submerged in the Lake. Depending on precipitation, the Lake level may again drop exposing the spring.

This hot spring is on State property because it is a part of the Mono Lake Tufa Reserve. The State does not want people to know about the spring. The reason:   nude bathers have offended visiting tourists. Prior to the submergence of the spring,  bathers were not allowed to use the spring during summer. High bacteria count was given as the excuse.

I enjoy visiting Navy Beach, especially around sunset. It's like visiting the ocean; there is the strong smell of salt in the air. And usually there's a good breeze off the water.

Stay on the main roads while visiting the Tufa Reserve. Be careful not to get stuck in the pumice sand. Two wheel drive cars and trucks can get stuck easily. Stay on the main road.

I remember one night, a friend and I who were singing at Whisky Creek at Mammoth Lakes, got the bright idea to go to Hawthorne, Nevada to gamble. This was like 2:30 in the morning. So we took off in a little Toyota. Going down Pole Line Road north of Mono Lake, we got another bright idea: Let's stop and look at the stars. So we pulled to the side of the road, right into the pumice sand. We got out and admired the beautiful night Sierra sky. Got back in and tried to drive but we were stuck.

To make a long story short, we slept in the car that night. The following morning someone with a truck and a tow chain hauled us out.

If you do get stuck in the pumice sand, deflate your tires slightly so that they are broader where they meet the sand. Then, with someone pushing from behind, gently ease your way out.

**Paoha Island Hot Spring**
**Location:** In Hot Springs Cove on Paoha Island in the middle of Mono Lake.
**Directions:** Get a boat and head out to Paoha Island, the larger island.
**Seclusion:** More seclusion than any normal human being could want.
**Fee:** You gotta be kidding.
**Temperature:** The source is something like 180 degrees Fahrenheit.
**Extraordinarily dangerous.**
**Condition:** Hot spring water flows into the lake. Old timers used to bathe out here. Primitive to say the least.
**Camping:** Sure, you can camp on the island, *but not during the nesting season.*
**George's 2 cents:** The islands are off limits during the summer when the seagulls are nesting. I'll be honest with you, I have not visited the Island nor the hot springs. But I've heard stories about men boiling eggs in them. If you attempt to reach Paoha Island by boat or otherwise, be certain to wear a life jacket. Even if the day is clear and the water is placid, Mono Lake can turn into a raging sea without notice. Several people lost their lives on the lake not long ago. Be careful and be safe. Let someone know where you are going and when you intend to return. Bring plenty of fresh water and food. There are no convenience stores on Paoha Island.

**Mammoth Lakes Hot Springs**

**Red's Meadow Hot Spring**
**Location:** Near Red's Meadow campground.
**Directions:** In Mammoth, from the corner of CA 203 and Old Mammoth Rd., drive west on 203, 5 miles to Mammoth Mountain Ski Resort. Continue on the road past the resort to Minaret Vista. Drive down the one lane road 7.6 miles to Red's Meadow Campground.
**Seclusion:** There are six private rooms.
**Fee:** None for hot spring.
**Temperature:** Flows out of the ground at over 125 degrees F..

**The bathhouse at Red's Meadow Campground near Mammoth Lakes. A very popular place during the summer season.**

**Condition:** Clean cement tubs.
**Camping:** Yes, at nearby Red's Meadow campground.
**George's 2 cents:** Hot mineral water is piped into the bath house for visitor use Memorial Day to Labor Day. The hot water is used during this time to heat the showers and the six private bath tubs in the campground. Baths are available on a first come basis. A metal grate covers the hot spring during summer. When the summer season is over, the metal grate is sometimes taken off and the hot spring is used by locals, cross country skiers or hikers. Check with the Forest Service about this before making the long trek in winter. The campground closes down around the end of October. In winter when the snow hits you must hike or cross country ski to reach the hot spring. And if you head out to the spring in winter, better tell someone where you are going and when you intend to return. The road from Minaret Vista is very steep, narrow and RV's are not advised.

**Fish Creek Hot Spring**
**Location:** 12 miles south of Red's Meadow campground.
**Directions:** From Red's Meadow campground, hike south on the Fish Creek Trail beyond Island Crossing in Fish Valley. Just past Sharktooth Creek Trail, cross the creek to Iva Bell Camp. The hot spring is about 100 yards up a path which passes through the campground. There are three pools.
**Seclusion:** Good.
**Fee:** None.
**Temperature:** About 110 degrees Fahrenheit.
**Condition:** Primitive but nice after a long hike.
**Camping:** Yes, nearby.
**George's 2 cents:** I did not hike 12 miles to inspect this hot spring. However, I did interview a person who has visited the hot spring several times. The directions come from him. So if they're wrong, I'll give you his name so you can shoot him or something.

Fish Creek Hot Spring is a fine place to relax after a long hike. The only thing wrong with this place is that you can't drive to it. So I'm not an environmental freak. Oh, I'm lying. I'm glad there isn't a road to this place. Have fun when you find it and send me a black and white picture. I need one for the revised edition of this book.


**Long Valley Hot Springs**
The Long Valley hot springs are a group of hot springs located in the Crowley Lake area south of Mammoth Lakes. The locations of the hot springs are mostly known only to locals. Therefore, fewer people visit. There are times during the day and the year when you can visit these and have them all to yourself. Spring and summer are the busiest times.


**Whitmore Hot Spring Pool**
**Location:** One mile east of U.S. Highway 395 at a point 9 miles south of Mammoth Lakes.
**Directions:** Take U.S. Highway 395 from Bishop north toward Mammoth Lakes. About 31 miles from Bishop you'll see a small green church on your right and a road sign, "Whitmore." This is Benton Crossing Road. Turn right here, east, and go one mile to

Whitmore.
**Seclusion:** This is a public swimming pool. Clothing required.
**Fee:** Yes.
**Open:** In summer only.
**Temperature:** Usually around 89 degrees Fahrenheit.
**Condition:** This is a concrete pool. Rest rooms are available.
**Camping:** Not at the pool but there are plenty of public lands nearby where you can camp. Owens River is only 4 miles east of here. Benton Crossing is a popular place to fish and camp. Brown's campground is located here; Brown's charges a small fee for camping. There's a store, rest rooms but no gas station.
**George's 2 cents:** If you have children and are looking for a clean, safe place, this is it. Seems not to get crowded even in summer. There is a Jacuzzi size tub at the southeast corner behind the pool. This is where water from the pool flows out in a narrow stream. The stream is shallow enough for kids to enjoy. There are other hot springs in the nearby area more secluded where there is no fee.

**Whitmore Pool near Mammoth Lakes is a good place for a swim.**

**Hot Creek**

**Location:** About 8 miles southeast of Mammoth Lakes near the airport.

**Directions:** Just north of the Mammoth Lakes airport on U.S. Highway 395, a paved road leads east to the Hot Creek Fish Hatchery. Follow this paved road and then turn right, or south, and follow the road behind the airport. You'll come to a dirt road that goes southeast to Hot Creek. Turn left at the dirt road and follow it two miles. You'll come to a parking lot where other cars are parked. You walk down a steep path to Hot Creek. It's quite a hike for the elderly or feeble.

**Seclusion:** This is a popular public place operated by the Forest Service. Clothing is required.

**Fee:** No.

**Accessibility:** You may have to hike or ski in in winter.

**Open:** All year from sunrise until sunset.

**Temperature:** Varies from hot to cold depending upon what part of the creek you're in.

**Rest rooms:** Yes.

**Condition:** Hot Creek is a "hot creek." Nice, but highly visited.

**Camping:** No way. It's on U.S. Forest Service land. Why would *they* allow you to camp on *your* land?

**George's 2 cents:** Hot Creek is one of the most popular places to visit in the Mammoth Lakes region. Many tourists visit. It's one of the places I take my friends who haven't visited the Eastern Sierra. It's a nice recreation spot if you have a family, easy to reach and fun if you like a small crowd. A ranger watches over the facility to protect and help the public. Hot Creek can be dangerous—even deadly. There are areas where there is scalding, violently hot water. These areas have been fenced off by the Forest Service. A number of people have been killed at Hot Creek in the last decade by venturing into the scalding water zones. But if you stay in the general bathing area, you should be OK. Even here, though, there are hot spots. Be careful.

## Long Valley Hot Springs

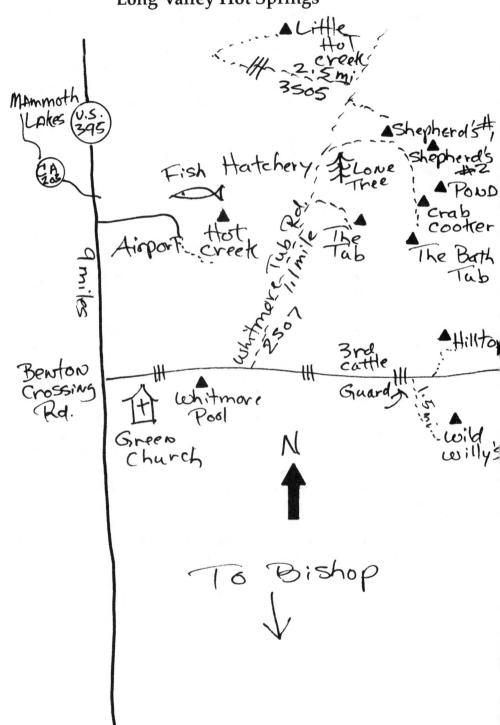

Top, Hot Creek near Mammtoth Lakes is a popular place in summer. Below, the dangers at Hot Creek are very real.

**A lovely large concrete tub has been built beside Little Hot Creek.**

**Little Hot Creek**
**Location:** In Long Valley near Mammoth Lakes about 1 mile north of Hot Creek.
**Directions:** At the green church on U.S. Highway 395 mentioned above, turn east and take Benton Crossing Road 1.2 miles until you come to a dirt road on your left, which should be posted Forest Service road 2S07, also known as Whitmore Tub Road. There may not be a road sign. Turn left here and follow this road until you come to another dirt road on your left marked 3S05. It's a few miles. A road will point the way to "Antelope Valley." Take this road 2.5 miles to the second cattle guard. Here, turn right and go 1 mile down a winding dirt road to Little Hot Creek Springs. A second route is to turn left on Whitmore Tub Road and drive 6.6 miles. You will come to a dirt road on your left. Turn left and drive 1.9 miles to the tub.
**Seclusion:** I've never seen anyone here when I've visited.
**Accessibility:** May be impossible to reach in winter even with 4-wheel drive. Cross country skiing may be the answer.

**Fee:** None.

**Temperature:** Let's put it this way: the source is boiling water.

**Condition:** A group of hot springs pour a hefty stream of water into a creek. There are several dams where pools are located. The farther you go down stream, the cooler the pools become. The bottom of the creek can be a bit mucky. Good suggestion is to bring a garden rake so you can clean out some of the green goo that grows here.

**Camping:** Well, it's on U.S. Forest Service land so you may have to ask *them* if you may use *your* land. Chances are you'll get a fat "No!"

**George's 2 cents:** Locals recently built a wonderful, large concrete tub beside the creek. This tub is used less than other Long Valley tubs. But please be aware: the source of this creek is scalding, dangerous water. The Forest Service has fenced this section off. Children should not be allowed by themselves near the source. Go down stream and be safe.

## Wild Willy's Hot Spring

**Location:** In Long Valley near Mammoth Lakes on a dirt road north of Crowley Lake.

**Directions:** Take U.S. Highway 395 from Bishop north toward Mammoth Lakes. At Benton Crossing Road (that's where that green church is) turn east. Drive 3.1 miles. Look for cattle guards. These are steel grates that cut across the road and make a heck of a racket when you drive over them. Count the cattle guards as you cross them. Exactly at the third cattle guard, 3.1 miles from U.S. Highway 395, there is a dirt road that goes to your right, to the south. Take this road and follow it 1.1 mile. You'll come to a parking area lined with boulders. Park and walk one half mile east.

**Seclusion:** Best times for private bathing are in the early morning and around 4-5 PM in the summer. Fewer people in the fall and winter. Weekends tend to be busy.

**Accessibility:** You'll need 4-wheel drive in winter.

**Temperature:** About 95 degrees Fahrenheit. The source is between 105-10 degrees Fahrenheit.

**Condition:** Good. There are two pools. A large concrete pool was made by locals. This pool is about 12 feet by 8. There are even

**Wild Willy'sHot Spring near Crowley Lake is a great place to soak.**

concrete benches where you can sit and a wooden deck for sun
bathing. The water is about hip deep. The floor of the pool is sand and
rock. Another smaller pool is nearby.

**Camping:** Camping is allowed at this time. Please do not camp next
to the spring. A good site is on the hilltop above the spring. Expect
rowdy partiers on weekends.

**Fee:** None.

**George's 2 cents:** This is one of our family's favorite hot springs. Our
children can play in the water by themselves and we can easily keep
our eyes on them. They are told not to jump or dive in the shallow
water. Weekends tend to draw more visitors. Many visitors prefer
to bathe nude. The BLM recently put up a road block and you can no
longer drive to the spring. Now you have to walk about a 1/2 mile.
They say this is to protect the meadow. However cattle are allowed
to stomp all over the meadow as much as they want. Strange when
cows have more rights than U.S. citizens. Unhappy about this? Call
the BLM at (760) 872-4881 and give them hell. The squeaky wheel gets

**Hilltop Hot Spring in Long Valley near Wild Willy's Hot Spring.**

the grease. These are the same clowns who stopped camping at Travertine Hot Spring near Bridgeport. Why? Oh, they just felt like it. Remember, you own your federal lands. Remind the boys.

### Hilltop Hot Spring Pool

**Location:** In Long Valley north of Crowley Lake not far from Wild Willy's Hot Spring.

**Directions:** If driving north from Bishop, go 31 miles to the green church at Benton Crossing Road. Turn right, go east, and drive 3.4 miles until you come to a dirt road on your left (north). Turn in and drive 1/4 mile and park. Follow the path and walk east up the hill to Hilltop Hot Spring. In winter you can hike across the meadow or cross-country ski from the road. It's only about 1/4 mile from the road.

**Seclusion:** Best times for private bathing are early in the morning and around 5 in the evening. Fewer visitors in fall and winter.

**Accessibility:** Good, right off Owens River road.

**Temperature:** Source is 125 degrees Fahrenheit; about 100 F. in the pool. Temperature in the pool can be changed by fiddling with sources of water. Plastic pipes bring both hot and cold water to the pool.

**Condition:** Excellent. This is a Jacuzzi size concrete pool with a drain for cleaning. Two pipes bring hot and cold water to the pool. You have to monkey with them sometimes to get the right temperature. Often in summer, locals drain the pool after each use. The reason: cattle are allowed to roam around here and they naturally will gather at the pool and drink from it. Problem is, they create quite a mess, if you get my drift.

**Camping:** Nope. It's located on land owned by those friendly folks at the Los Angeles Department of Water and Power.

**Fee:** No.

**George's 2 cents:** It's a very nice spot. Easy to reach and usually, fewer people. The view of the mountains and valley is spectacular. Nice place to take the one you love for an afternoon picnic.

**The Tub Hot Spring**

**Location:** In Long Valley about 1/2 mile north of Benton Crossing Road not far from Wild Willy's.

**Directions:** Again, if you are approaching from Bishop or Mammoth, take Benton Crossing Road at the green church (9 miles south of Mammoth Lakes turnoff) and head east 1.2 miles until you come to a dirt road on your left, Whitmore Tub Road. Turn left onto the dirt road. Follow it for about 1.2 miles. You will come to a dirt road on your right. Turn right. Follow it 200 yards to the hot spring.

**Seclusion:** This hot spring is visited less than Wild Willy's but it is still popular with locals and others. A good time for private bathing is in the early morning before 10 AM and around 4 in the afternoon.

**Accessibility:** You will need 4-wheel drive in winter.

**Fee:** No.

**Temperature:** Source is 120 degrees Fahrenheit. You can regulate the water flow into the tub, and therefore the temperature.

**Condition:** Good. A concrete tub about the size of Jacuzzi is fed by a hose attached to the hot water source about 100 yards away. Occasionally needs cleaning out. This is done by removing the PVC

**Kids enjoy a soak in the waist deep Tub Hot Spring.**

pipe and allowing the water to drain. Then scrub the tub clean with a brush and bleach. Then put the PVC pipe back in and let the tub fill up. Takes about 2 hours to fill.

**Camping:** Yes, for the time being. Do not camp right next to the tub.

**George's 2 cents:** This is my second favorite hot spring in Long Valley. This tub is smaller than Wild Willy's and more intimate. Some folks bathe here in the evening, camp at night, and bathe again in the morning before hitting the road. I've camped here often with my family. By the way, if you have an AC/DC TV, you can pick up the networks by using UHF. There's a translator on one of the mountains to the east.

### Shepherd's Hot Spring (Lone Tree)
**Location:** In Long Valley about 1 mile north of The Tub.

**Directions:** Take Benton Crossing Road 1.2 miles to the first dirt road on your left, Forest Service Road 2S07, also known as Whitmore Tub Road. There may not be a road sign at this intersection. Turn left

**Shepherd's Hot Spring in Long Valley near Crowley Lake.**

onto this road and drive 1.9 miles until you see a lone tree on your
right. Turn right onto the dirt road just before the tree. Follow it for
a 1/4 mile. Where the road forks, go left. You will come to a little
valley where there is a pond in wet years, or a dry lake in dry years.
The hot spring is just this side of the pond.

**Accessibility:** You'll need 4-wheel drive in winter when it snows.

**Seclusion:** Visited less than the other Long Valley hot springs. Best
times early in the morning and in the afternoon around 4. Fewer
people in fall and winter.

**Fee:** No.

**Temperature:** Water flows from a small pond at 113 degrees Fahrenheit. You can cool the tub by diverting the hot water.

**Condition:** Good. This is a small man made concrete tub. Four can fit
in comfortably.

**Camping:** Yes, about one hundred yards west on BLM land. The tub
is located on land owned by the Los Angeles Department of Water
and Power.

**Shepherd's Hot Spring #2 is one of the new tubs in the Long Valley area. It has both a hot and cold water source.**

**George's 2 cents:** This tub was supposedly made by shepherds, hence, Shepherd's Hot Spring. This is a good spot if you want more seclusion and a little hotter water. Water may get too hot in the summer when the sun heats the water in the pond that feeds the spring. To cool tub, move pipe away from tub and let water cool. Nice place to camp too.

**Shepherd's Hot Spring #2**
**Location:** In Long Valley about 1/4 mile east of Shepherd's Tub.
**Directions:** Take Benton Crossing Road 1.2 miles to the first dirt road on your left, Forest Service Road 2S07, also known as Whitmore Tub Road. There may not be a road sign at this intersection. Turn left onto this road and drive 1.9 miles until you see a lone tree on your right. Turn right onto the dirt road just before the tree. Follow it for 1/2 mile. You will come to a small parking lot lined with rocks. Follow a trail around the left side of the knoll down the hill about 100 yards

to the tub.

**Accessibility:** Good. But you may need 4-wheel drive in winter when it snows.

**Seclusion:** Visited less than  other Long Valley hot springs. Best times early in the morning and in the afternoon around 4 p.m. Fewer people in fall and winter.

**Fee:** No.

**Temperature:** There are two pipes bringing in both hot and cold water. You can vary the temperature as you like.

**Condition:** Really nice concrete pool in the shape of a jacuzzi that can fit about 8 people.

**Camping:** Yes, back up the road on  BLM land near Shepherd's Tub. However, there is some dispute as what land out here is LA's and what is BLM  land. Even BLM and the LA DWP don't know the boundaries. So you camp at some risk. In the last few years LA DWP has been posting No Camping signs in the area. I usually pick a spot to camp where there isn't a No Camping sign.

**George's 2 cents:** This is one of the more recently built tubs in the area. Whoever made this tub knew what they were doing. They engineered pipes to  both hot and cold water springs which makes it easy to control the temperature in the tub. This tub appears to be less visited than others in the area.

### The Crab Cooker (Ken's tub)

**Location:** 1/2 mile south of Shepherd's Hot Spring.

**Directions:** From Shepherd's Hot Spring, walk or drive south on the dirt road 1/2 mile. Road leads into a tiny valley circled on three sides by hills. The Crab Cooker is located here.

**Seclusion:** Best times are fall and winter. Although this is a fairly new tub, it has become popular with locals and others.

**Accessibility:** Good, except in winter. Roads out here are not plowed.

**Temperature:** The source is boiling water. Hence the name "crab cooker." The source has been covered by a metal grate now.

**Condition:** A wonderfully made Jacuzzi-size concrete tub. Flow of hot water can be controlled by a valve. To get the water to flow faster, move the drain pipe just a bit to allow the water to slowly drain. This helps to suck in the water from the source.

**Camping:** Camping was allowed until recently. Site is on LA

**Crab Cooker is just around the corner from Shepherd's.**

Department of Water land. Now a cop patrols the area and keeps people from camping.

**Fee:** None.

**George's 2 cents:** Until recently, this was a wonderful place to camp. The Los Angeles Department of Water and Power fixed that by posting "No camping" signs. Why? I guess people were having too much fun and not bothering anyone. Go figure.

**The Bath Tub**

**Location:** In a gully southwest of the Crab Cooker 300 yards.

**Directions:** Follow the path from the Crab Cooker southwest and up the hillside about 300 yards to a gully below rocky cliffs.

**Seclusion:** Excellent.

**Accessibility:** If there ain't no snow and you can walk, you've got it made.

**Temperature:** About 90 degrees Fahrenheit.

**Condition:** Well, there was a bath tub here until recently when

someone swiped it. Whoever did it, bring it back or I will find you and eat you. Now there is a small little pool of sand and rock. Great place for a quick bath. Avoid using soap. Don't give the LA Department of Water and Power any excuse for shutting the place down.
**Camping:** Not anymore. This is LA Department of Water land.
**Fee:** None.
**George's 2 cents:** Nice place for a bath and to sit back and soak in the sun.

### The Pond Hot Spring
**Location:** 1/2 mile southeast of Shepherd's hot spring.
**Directions:** From Shepherd's Hot Spring, walk or drive a half mile south on a dirt road. Look to your left, to the east. You'll see a pond down the hill in a valley. In the morning or in the evening you may see wisps of steam coming from the pond. The hot spring pond is located at the western edge of the pond. The hot spring is likely the source for the pond.
**Seclusion:** If you don't mind walking through some slushy grasslands, you can have this place to yourself.
**Fee:** Are you kidding?
**Temperature:** About 90 degrees Fahrenheit.
**Camping:** No.
**George's 2 cents:** Well, when I visited this place in the spring, it was mucky getting out to it. Water is shallow, about knee deep. If you're really hard-up for a hot spring, this could be fun.

### Old House Benton Hot Springs
**Phone:** (760) 933-2507
**Web site:** www.395.com/oldhouse
**Location:** 4 miles west of Benton, California.
**Address:** Rt. 4 Box 58 , Benton, CA 93512
**Directions:** From Bishop, take Highway 6, 30 miles to Benton. At Benton, take Highway 120, 4 miles west to Old Benton Hot Springs. You can also reach Benton Hot Springs from Mammoth Lakes by taking Benton CrossingRoad 9 miles south of Mammoth Lakes turnoff on U.S. 395 and following the paved road until it turns into a graded dirt road. Follow this road for about 23.6 miles to Highway 120. Then go east, or turn right, 4 miles to Old Benton Hot Springs.

**The Pond Hot Spring can be seen from Shepherd's Hot Spring#2 looking east. Look for vapor rising from the pond on a cold morning.**

**Seclusion:** Yes. 4 private outdoor tubs which are secluded one from the other.
**Fee:** $7 per hour per person; $12 per couple per hour.
**Temperature:** Approximately 101 degrees Fahrenheit in the tubs. Water temperatures can be adjusted as you wish. The source is between 130-40 degrees Fahrenheit.
**Condition:** Recently built 4 redwood outdoor tubs about five feet in diameter with concrete bottoms, 3-4 feet deep. Tub water is changed after every use and tubs are sanitized.
**Camping/Lodging:** Camping $10 per person up to about 5 people. Dry camp only. RV' o.k. but no hook-ups. Lodging at the Bed and Breakfast or Inn is $69 double with use of hot springs and full breakfast all year.
**George's 2 cents:** Four redwood tubs are located outdoors. You can tent camp next to the tubs. There is RV camping but there are no hookups. Clothing optional. The General Store at Old Benton has

**Taking a  soak in one of the new redwood tubs at Old House Benton Hot Springs at Benton**

been closed. The Old House is open 24 hours. Manager lives next door in RV. He says just knock on his door for help. The Old House has a small supply of snacks, ice cream and sodas.  Benton Hot Springs, or Old Benton, was originally a silver mining town in the 1860's. It's a nice quiet place in the sticks. Can get hot out here in the summer though. Spring and fall are nice.

**Keough's Hot Spring**
**Phone:** (760) 872-4670
**Location:** Located half way between Big Pine and Bishop, about 8 miles south of Bishop.
**Directions:** From the corner of U.S. 395 and East Line Street in Bishop, drive south on U.S. Highway 395, 7.4 miles. Look for a road sign that points west to Keough's Hot Spring. Turn right at Keough's Hot Spring Road and drive .5  mile west to the clubhouse.

**Keough's Hot Springs near Bishop.**

**Seclusion:** This is a public place.

**Temperature:** There are two swimming pools. One larger pool is kept at around 90 degrees Fahrenheit; the second smaller pool at about 104 degrees Fahrenheit.

**Open:** All year. Summer hours Monday thru Thursday 9 a.m.-8 p.m. Friday and Saturday 9 a.m.-9 p.m.. Sunday 9 a.m.-7 p.m. Winter Hours are from 11 a.m. -7 p.m. Closed on Tuesdays.

**Condition:** 2 concrete pools. Rest rooms and changing rooms are available.

**Fee:** Day use $7 for adults; $5 for children 12 and under.

**Camping:** No tent camping. Partial RV hookups. Self-contained RV's $19 a nite with water and electricity; $16 for a dry site.

**George's 2 cents:** Three hot springs with a huge flow of water emerge at the bottom of the eastern wall of the Sierra Nevada about 8 miles south of Bishop. The mineral water is piped into pools located behind wooden walls. You must sign a disclaimer to use the pool if no lifeguard is on duty. During the summer there is a life guard.

**Keough's Hot Spring Ditch has some wonderful deep pools for soaking. Easy to reach right off the highway.**

### Keough's Hot Spring Ditch
**Location:** Just below Keough's Hot Spring on a dirt road.
**Directions:** From Bishop drive 7 miles south on U.S. 395. Turn right at Keough's Hot Spring Road and drive 1/2 mile, then turn right on a dirt road just before Keough's Hot Spring resort. Go 1/4 mile.
**Seclusion:** This place is highly visited.
**Temperature:** Around 110 degrees Fahrenheit at the southern end of the ditch; cools to around 95 degrees Fahrenheit as the water flows north down the ditch.
**Condition:** Rock dams help to hold in the hot water and make pools with sandy bottoms.
**Fee:** No.
**Camping:** I was told in a letter by those loving and generous folks at the Los Angeles Department of Water and Power that camping is not allowed here. Why? You figure it out. Apparently DWP owns the land. These are the same people who are responsible for the robbery

and rape of the Owens Valley. Four thousand American farmers in the Owens Valley saw their farms and homes destroyed by the greed and maliciousness of the City of Los Angeles. All this to get their hands on the Owens River which today is the main source of fresh water for the City of Los Angeles. Could this be why Los Angeles today is such a non-violent, clean and friendly place? Poetic justice. **George's 2 cents:** Keough's Hot Spring Ditch is free and it's just off the highway. It's a nice place to stop on a long trip through Owens Valley. If you follow the ditch as it winds north, you will find several deep pools. Nice place to picnic. Last time I visited I saw a lot of trash. Please take out what you bring in. If you trash this place, the LA Department of Water and Power could shut it down. Please do what you can to keep the place clean and pick up trash if the spirit moves you. There's some broken glass around the area. Warn the children. Expect party types on weekends.

**THE REDLIGHT LADIES OF VIRGINIA CITY, NEVADA** Virginia City was the richest mining camp in the American West. The silver from its mines built San Francisco and helped the Union win the Civil War. From 1860-95, Virginia City had three of the largest redlight districts in America. Here women from around the world worked the world's oldest profession. Author Williams tells the stories of the strange lives of the redlight girls, their legends and violent deaths. Based on newspaper accounts, county records and U.S. Census information. Perhaps the best and most informative book on prostitution in the old West. Plenty of historic photos, illustrations, map and letters. 48 pages. AUTOGRAPHED. $6.95 quality paperback.

**THE GUIDE TO BODIE AND EASTERN SIERRA HISTORIC SITES** True story of the rise and fall of Bodie, California's most famous mining camp, today a ghost town, National Historic Site and California State Park. Known as the toughest gold mining town in the West where millions were made in a few years, murders were a daily occurrence. Has a beautiful full color cover with 100 photos on an 8 1/2 X 11 format. 88 pages. AUTOGRAPHED. $12.95 quality paperback.

**THE MURDERS AT CONVICT LAKE** True story of the infamous 1871 Nevada State Penitentiary break in which 29 outlaws escaped and fled more than 250 miles into Mono and Inyo counties, California. They vowed to kill anyone who got in their way. In a terrible shootout at Monte Diablo, today known as Convict Lake just south of Mammoth Lakes ski resort, the convicts killed two men. They fled to nearby Bishop where they were captured and hanged. Includes 18 rare photographs and pen and ink drawings by Dave Comstock. 32 pages. AUTOGRAPHED. $5.95 quality paperback.

**MARK TWAIN: HIS ADVENTURES AT AURORA AND MONO LAKE** When Sam Clemens arrived in Nevada in 1861, he wanted to get rich quick. He tried silver mining at Aurora, Nevada near Mono Lake not far from Yosemite National Park. Clemens didn't strike it rich but his hard luck mining days led to his literary career. 32 rare photos, mining deeds and maps to places where Clemens lived, wrote, camped. 100 pages. AUTOGRAPHED. $6.95 paper.

**MARK TWAIN: HIS LIFE IN VIRGINIA CITY, NEVADA** While reporting for the *Territorial Enterprise* in Virginia City, 1862-64, Sam Clemens adopted his well known pen name, Mark Twain. Here is the lively account of Mark Twain's early writing days in the most exciting town in the West. Over 60 rare photos and maps to places Twain lived and wrote. 208 pages. AUTOGRAPHED. $10.95 quality paper.

**MARK TWAIN AND THE JUMPING FROG OF CALAVERAS COUNTY** The true story of Twain's discovery of "The Celebrated Jumping Frog of Calaveras County," the publication of which launched his international career. After getting run out of Virginia City, Twain settled in San Francisco in May, 1864. After a discouraging prospecting trip, in a saloon at Angel's Camp, Twain was told the Jumping Frog story by a bartender. Twain's version, published eleven months later, became an international hit. "The Celebrated Jumping Frog of Calaveras County," is included in this book. 116 pages, index, bibliography, 35 historic photographs, guide maps for travelers. AUTOGRAPHED. Quality paper $8.95.

**New ! ON THE ROAD WITH MARK TWAIN IN CALIFORNIA AND NEVADA** Here is a handy, easy to read guide to Mark Twain's haunts in California and Nevada 1861-68. Has road directions to historic sites, guide maps and 100 photographs of Twain, historic sites and Twain's friends. Gives brief run-downs of each place and tells what Twain was doing while there. A must-have book for any Twain fan who would like to follow his trail in the far West. 136 pages, 100 photos, road maps, index. $16.95 pap.; $29.95 hard cover. AUTOGRAPHED.

**THE SONGWRITER'S DEMO MANUAL AND SUCCESS GUIDE** shows the songwriter and aspiring group how to make a professional demo tape at home or in the studio and how to use it to sell songs and land record deals. Williams explains how the music business operates, who the important people are and how to make contact with them. 200 pages, photos and illustrations and complete resource Appendix. $29.95 Library edition. AUTOGRAPHED.

# Order Form

Name_____

Address_____City_____

State_____Zip_____

E mail address_____

Yes, George send me the following books, autographed and inscribed:

___Copy(ies) Hot Springs of Northern California, 12.95 pap.
___Copy(ies) Hot Springs of the Eastern Sierra, 10.95 pap.
___Copy(ies) Hot Springs of Nevada, 10.95 pap.
___Copy(ies) In the Last of the Wild West, 12.95 pap.
___Copy(ies) Rosa May: The Search For A Mining Camp Legend,
             10.95 pap.
___Copy(ies) The Redlight Ladies of Virginia City, 6.95 pap.
___Copy(ies) The Guide to Bodie, 12.95 pap.
___Copy(ies) The Murders at Convict Lake, 6.95 pap.
___Copy(ies) Mark Twain: His Adventures at Aurora, 8.95 pap.
___Copy(ies) Mark Twain: His Life In Virginia City, Nevada,
             10.95 pap.
___Copy(ies) Mark Twain and the Jumping Frog, 8.95 pap.
___Copy(ies) On the Road with Mark Twain In California and
             Nevada, 16.95 pap.; 29.95 hard cover
___Copy(ies) The Songwriter's Demo Manual, $29.95 hard cover.
___Copy(ies) Repair Your Credit

Shipping by postal service is 2.25 for the first book, .75 each additional book. Faster shipping via Priority Mail is 4.00 for the first book. 1.00 each additional book. Overnight Fed Express is $14 for a single book.

Total for books_____
Shipping        _____
Total enclosed in check or money order _____
Mail your order to:

**TBR Trust**
**P.O. Box 191**
**Genoa , Nevada 89411**

# Order Form

Name_____

Address_____City_____

State_____Zip_____

e mail address_____

Yes, George send me the following books, autographed and inscribed:

___Copy(ies) Hot Springs of Northern California, 12.95 pap.
___Copy(ies) Hot Springs of the Eastern Sierra, 10.95 pap.
___Copy(ies) Hot Springs of Nevada, 10.95 pap.
___Copy(ies) In the Last of the Wild West, 12.95 pap.
___Copy(ies) Rosa May: The Search For A Mining Camp Legend,
            10.95 pap.
___Copy(ies) The Redlight Ladies of Virginia City, 6.95 pap.
___Copy(ies) The Guide to Bodie, 12.95 pap.
___Copy(ies) The Murders at Convict Lake, 6.95 pap.
___Copy(ies) Mark Twain: His Adventures at Aurora, 8.95 pap.
___Copy(ies) Mark Twain: His Life In Virginia City, Nevada,
            10.95 pap.
___Copy(ies) Mark Twain and the Jumping Frog, 8.95 pap.
___Copy(ies) On the Road with Mark Twain In California and
            Nevada, 16.95 pap.; 29.95 hard cover
___Copy(ies) The Songwriter's Demo Manual, $29.95 hard cover.
___Copy(ies) Repair Your Credit

Shipping by postal service is 2.25 for the first book, .75 each additional book. Faster shipping via Priority Mail is 4.00 for the first book. 1.00 each additional book. Overnight Fed Express is $14 for a single book.

Total for books_____
Shipping        _____
Total enclosed in check or money order _____
Mail your order to:

**TBR Trust**
**P.O. Box 191**
**Genoa , Nevada 89411**